Starting Out Right With Your New Cat

ALSO BY KIM CAMPBELL THORNTON:

The Complete Idiot's Guide To Beagles, Alpha, 2003
Simple Solutions: Aggression, Bowtie Press, 2003
Simple Solutions: Housetraining, Bowtie Press, 2003
Simple Solutions: Obedience, Bowtie Press, 2003
Simple Solutions: Barking, Bowtie Press, 2002
Simple Solutions: Chewing, Bowtie Press, 2002
Simple Solutions: Digging, Bowtie Press, 2002
Mastiffs: A Complete Pet Owner's Manual, Barron's, 1999
Bloodhounds: A Complete Pet Owner's Manual, Barron's, 1998
Why Do Cats Do That?, Bowtie Press, 1998
Cat Treats, Doubleday, 1997

innova publishing

Starting Out Right With

Your New Cat

A Complete Guide

KIM CAMPBELL THORNTON

For Shelby, Peter, Pandora, and the next New Cat

innova publishing
37 West 20th Street, Suite 1108
New York, NY 10011

Starting Out Right With Your New Cat

LCCN: 2004108240
ISBN: 0974937347

This book has also been published under the title *Your New Cat*

Published by arrangement with Capital Books, Inc.

Manufactured in the United States of America on acid-free paper

10   9   8   7   6   5   4   3   2   1

Contents

Acknowledgments

The author would like to thank the following cat lovers for their help with the information in this book: Janine Adams; Darlene Arden; Margaret H. Bonham; Michael Brim; Steve Dale; Donna Day; Linda Donaldson; Deb M. Eldredge, DVM; Lexiann Grant-Snyder; John Hamil, DVM; J. Anne Helgren; Lynn Hofstetter; Jean Hofve, DVM; Amy Marder, VMD; John McGonagle; Alice Moon-Fanelli, PhD; Brook Niemiec, DVM; Carolyn Osier; Jill A. Richardson, DVM; Amy D. Shojai; Carolyn Vella; and Bob Walker.

Introduction

When my husband and I got married, some twenty years ago, one of the first things we did was acquire two kittens. We both loved cats, and knew we would enjoy their company. We knew only a minimum of cat care—how much could there be to know, anyway?—enough to have them both spayed so there wouldn't be any unwanted kittens and enough to train them to come to a whistle.

Three years later I was hired as an assistant editor at *Cat Fancy* magazine. Every week I brought home books and articles about cat care, behavior, and health. Like cats rolling in catnip, we reveled in the new insights we were gaining about our animals. We went from an elementary education in feline culture to graduate-level study, and our cats benefited.

They went from eating cheap cat food to eating premium cat food. The difference could be seen in their coats and in their level of health. When we caught them eyeing a skunk in our backyard, that was the end of their forays outdoors—no more worries about diseases, fights, or eau de skunk. We became keen observers of the feline condition, learning to recognize problems early, before they became serious.

Since those first two cats, we have shared our home with five more cats. Of the seven, three died young of diseases that weren't preventable at the time, although keeping them indoors certainly might have helped hinder exposure. One, to our sorrow, was hit by a car in the years before we began our education in cats. One developed diabetes at the age of five, but with good care managed to live until the ripe old age of fifteen. Two we still have: one is fifteen and one is nineteen. Proof positive that our study of feliculture has paid off in long-term relationships with these special cats.

Still, we regret all that we didn't know in the beginning. Along the way, we made mistakes with training, with care, with nutrition, with health. Cat ownership can be fraught with frustration when you don't know what you're doing or when your expectations are more—or less—than your cat can meet.

Whether you are getting a cat for companionship, or because you want a being to nurture, for rodent control, or for any other reason, you need to couple your expectations with practical, up-to-date knowledge and understanding of the feline psyche and physiology. Too often, people rely on outdated images of cats; for instance, that they're independent, solitary, and untrainable. We know now that cats can be trained, that cats need companionship and interactive play and intellectual challenges, that cats can love us not in the way that a human or a dog loves us but in their own unique catlike way.

As we all know, the best way to learn is by asking questions, and in this book, there's no such thing as a dumb question. Each chapter starts with a brief introduction about the subject, followed by related questions and answers. The book covers every aspect of finding and living with a cat, from the all-important, number one question—Do you really want a cat?—to dealing with the special needs of that cat fifteen or twenty years later during his geriatric years. In between, you'll find information about the best ways to acquire a cat, what you'll need before you bring your new cat home, recognizing and dealing with health and behavior problems, and socializing and training your cat.

What makes me qualified to write this book? In a word, experience. Beyond my stint at *Cat Fancy* (and its sister publication, *Dog Fancy*), I'm now a journalist who specializes in writing about animal care and companionship. I write articles and books on pet care, many of which have been honored with awards from the Cat Writers' Association and the Dog Writers Association of America. Those first two cats are no longer with me, but I think about them often and thank them for setting my feet on the road to feline higher education. They and the other animals who have shared my life have taught me much along the way.

In this book, you'll notice that I use personal pronouns—*he* or *she*—when I talk about cats. Sometimes this is because it's appropriate to the discussions at hand—spaying or neutering, for instance—but mainly it's because I believe our animals deserve the dignity of being referred to with gender-specific pronouns rather than the generic "it."

Finally, while this book is designed to provide you with all the information you need to start off right with your new cat, it's not meant to replace advice from other experts such as veterinarians and animal behaviorists. If the suggestions you find here don't work for you and your cat, or if you have a question that this book doesn't address, please seek help from your veterinarian or a specialist in feline behavior.

Whether with other people or with animals, it's when understanding is absent that relationships falter and even fall apart. I've written this book to help you learn about the myriad facets of cat care. The better you understand your cat, the deeper your relationship will become. And that's a very special thing.

CHAPTER 1

Making Sure You're Ready for a New Cat

L IFE WITH A CAT is a special adventure. The acquisition of this mewing ball of fluff is the beginning of a lifetime of fun and friendship. New cat owners can look forward to the antics of kittenhood, the fascination of watching a kitten develop into a cat, the soft batting of a paw on the face in the morning, and the pleasure of a purring cat in the lap. But there is more to cat ownership than just the good times. Indeed, this new relationship can be compared to a marriage. As a kitten becomes a cat, he learns the ins and outs of living with a human family. Family members, in turn, come to cherish the cat for his uniquely feline nature: an independent yet loving heart, a curiosity that knows no bounds, and a serenity that surely inspired Zen meditation.

Just as a new marriage requires maturity and commitment to a lifetime together, so does a relationship with a cat. The responsibility for the life of another creature, especially one as special as a cat, is not one to be taken lightly, to be tossed aside when it grows heavy. For better or for worse, the kitten or cat you choose should be with you for the entire span of his life—in sickness and in health—a period that could last twenty years or more.

There's no doubt that the relationship will have its bumpy spots. Learning to communicate with another species takes time. And effort. And patience. There are only so many times one can come home to shredded curtains without at least contemplating mayhem. And no doubt Kitten will wonder about this being who so haltingly communicates in Feline. Why doesn't she just say what she wants instead of shrieking and pulling her hair out?

But then it's time to kiss and make up; to renew the vows made to teach, care for, and love this feline life; to strengthen the fragile ties of a budding relationship. The rewards are immeasurable. A cat is always there, always listening, always a comfort, no matter what else has gone wrong. So as you prepare to enter into this special relationship, be aware of your new cat's needs: companionship, training, food, grooming, shelter, and veterinary care.

Companionship means spending time with your cat. It's true that cats sleep up to eighteen hours a day, but that doesn't mean that they thrive if constantly left alone. Cats left too much to their own devices can develop emotional or behavior problems. Companionship can be active—tossing a ping-pong ball for the cat to chase or dangling a fishing-pole toy—or passive, sitting with the cat in your lap while you watch television.

Training goes hand in paw with companionship. You might not teach your cat the same obedience commands you would a dog (although you could), but all cats need to know the basics of living in a household: don't scratch the furniture, don't get on the kitchen counter, do use the litter box, and so on. Training is also a great way to stimulate your cat's very bright mind. We don't often think of teaching cats tricks, but this kind of training helps keep them entertained, exercised, and out of trouble. You'll find information on play and training in chapters ten and twelve.

Of course you'll feed your cat, but there's more to it than simply buying what's on sale at the grocery store. Cats have specific nutritional needs, and a high-quality food is the best way to ensure that your cat enjoys nine long lives. Chapter eight offers advice on kitty eating habits, nutritional needs, and evaluating cat foods.

What about grooming? Don't cats bathe themselves? It's rare that you'll need to give a cat a bath, but regular brushing distributes skin oils for a healthy coat and removes dead hair that would otherwise get on clothing and furniture or be regurgitated in the form of a hairball. You'll also want to trim the nails on a regular basis, both for your protection and that of your furniture and clothing. See chapter nine for tips on grooming your cat.

Cats used to come and go at will, and no one ever thought of confining them to a house, but indoors is the safest place for your cat to be. Indoor cats live longer, because they're not exposed to disease or injury from other animals, cars, or people with malicious intent.

Naturally, your cat will need you to provide veterinary care. Besides taking her in for an annual exam and vaccinations as needed, you'll need to learn to recognize the signs that may indicate health problems. In chapter seven, you'll find information on the health issues that can affect cats and the physical signs and behaviors that should prompt a visit to the veterinarian.

With all of these things in mind, make a promise to yourself and to the kitten or cat you choose. Promise yourself that you will make every effort to choose wisely so that the association will be a happy one; and promise your cat that you will be a patient teacher and loving friend. Your cat will do his part. Together, the two of you will become a new link in the chain of cats and people who have shared lives over the past four thousand years.

To find out if you're ready for the unique challenge and pleasure of living with a cat, read on. The answers to the questions asked in this chapter will help you make that decision.

THE HOME-ALONE CAT

I'm single and work all day. Is a cat a good choice for me?

Cats have a reputation as solitary creatures. With the exception of lions, they generally live and hunt alone. Because of this, they're good candidates as companions for people who are at work or school during the day.

That said, how well cats do on their own depends on their individual personalities and their early environment. Some cat breeds are more people-oriented than others—Abyssinians, Siamese, and Burmese, for instance—and they're less likely to tolerate long periods of being alone. Other cats at risk of developing separation anxiety are orphaned kittens, kittens weaned too early, or kittens that didn't get enough socialization in the first weeks of life.

If you're concerned about your cat being alone during the day, you may want to consider getting two cats so they can keep each other company. Having two cats isn't always an option, but there are other steps you can take to keep your cat entertained while you're gone:

- Tune the television to a nature channel. Many cats enjoy watching television, especially when it shows their favorite prey animals: birds, squirrels, fish.
- Provide "live" entertainment with a window bird feeder.
- Leave out a variety of interactive toys such as squeaky mice, battery-operated motorized balls that move on their own, and toys enhanced with catnip and feathers. Rotate toys every few days so your cat doesn't get bored.
- For climbing fun, set up a floor-to-ceiling cat tree in an area where your cat can get a view of the great outdoors.

     No matter how well your cat is entertained during the day, make it a point to spend some time playing with or grooming her as soon as you get home.

THE INDOOR CAT

Does a cat need to go outside?

We like to think of cats as free-ranging animals that can take care of themselves. Nonetheless, they are domesticated animals that depend on us for care and food. Cats allowed to roam outdoors are exposed to diseases, attacks from other animals, injuries from cars, poisons such as snail or rodent bait, and harm from people who don't like cats. A cat that stays indoors avoids these risks.

Parasites are another problem for outdoor cats. They bring home fleas, ticks, and ear mites. The resulting itching, biting, and scratching isn't pretty, and it's really annoying when it occurs on the bed in the middle of the night. Parasite problems decrease dramatically when a cat stays indoors.

The bottom line? The average life span of an outdoor cat is three to five years, while the average life span of an indoor cat is twelve to sixteen years. Your cat will live a longer, healthier life if you keep him indoors.

Does that mean your cat can never go outside? Not at all. You can teach your cat to walk on a leash—yes, it can be done! You can build an enclosure in your yard where your cat can enjoy the outdoors without the risks, or you can permit supervised play in a fenced yard. To help prevent your cat from going over the fence, place chicken wire along the top so that it extends outward along the inside of the fence for about one foot.

DEALING WITH NO-PETS LEASES

I really want a cat, but my landlord doesn't allow pets. What can I do?

Your landlord probably has good reasons for not permitting pets. Many people are irresponsible, and they permit or don't prevent un-

With a little effort, your cat can enjoy the outdoors safely.

desirable behaviors such as scratching carpets or marking walls or other areas by spraying them with urine.

Whatever you do, don't try to sneak a cat onto the premises. Sooner or later, the cat will be discovered (cats love lying on windowsills and watching the world go by), and your new friend (and possibly you) will be evicted.

Instead, ask your landlord if there are any circumstances under which she might permit a cat. Explain the steps you would take to prevent damage to the apartment (scooping the litter box every day, disposing of waste and cat litter properly, providing an effective scratching post, and so on). If you've had a cat previously in an apartment, request a letter from that landlord stating that you were a responsible pet-owning tenant. Offer to pay a nonrefundable pet deposit or a small amount ($15 to $25) toward pet "rent" every month. You may also want to consider finding a new apartment that does allow pets.

FINDING KITTY-FRIENDLY RENTALS

We're moving to a new city. How can we find a rental unit that will permit us to have a cat?

Finding a rental that allows pets is much like the search for the perfect job. If you already have a cat, start by preparing a résumé for her. Chessie's résumé should summarize her best qualities and include examples of your responsibility as a pet owner. Elements to include are her age, activity level, health, and behavior. For instance: Chessie is a three-year-old spayed tuxedo cat with a sweet personality. When she's not lying in a sunny window, she loves scratching on and climbing her five-foot cat tree. She is an indoors-only cat who is litter-box-trained and up-to-date on her vaccinations.

Describe what steps you take to keep your cat and premises flea-free and how your cat is cared for when you're out of town. Other important items to include, if possible, are a letter from your current landlord stating that you are a responsible pet-owning tenant as well as a letter from your veterinarian, testifying to your good character as a cat owner. For tips on finding pet-friendly housing and examples of pet résumés, see the Web sites of the Humane Society of the United States at www.hsus.org/ace/457?searchstring=renting, the Animal Rescue League of Boston at www.arlboston.com, and the San Francisco SPCA (Society for the Prevention of Cruelty to Animals) at www.sfspca.org.

CATS FOR SENIORS

I am a senior citizen and live in federal housing. Would a cat be a good pet for me?

Cats are good companions for senior citizens because they're small and they don't require outdoor exercise like dogs. The U.S. Housing and Urban Development (HUD) department has a "Pets in Elderly Housing" regulation that applies to federally assisted rental housing designated exclusively for residency by people sixty-two years of age or older or people with disabilities. It allows all residents of most federally funded housing to have pets, including cats, although landlords may set rules that limit the number or size of pets. Be aware that this rule does not apply to people who use vouchers to secure housing on the private market. Some states, including California, Massachusetts, and New Jersey, have similar laws allowing pets in public housing for senior citizens or people with disabilities. If you live in city- or state-funded housing, check with the housing authority overseeing the program to find out if any regulations apply to cat ownership.

CATS AND KIDS

Are my children old enough for a cat?

A cat can be a great addition to a household no matter what age your children are. They need supervision, of course, any time they interact with children. A cat's attitude toward a baby can range from indifference to curiosity. It's all right for your cat to sniff the baby (that old wives' tale about cats sucking the breath from babies isn't true), but don't let your cat sleep with the baby or play with his toys. They each need their own space. Toddlers must be prevented from pulling the cat's tail, carrying him upside down, and generally making his life miserable. Teach young children how to pet the cat nicely, not to hold the cat too tightly, and not to pick the cat up.

It's a different question altogether if your child is asking for a cat of her own. Your child should be at least six years old and capable of participating in the cat's care before you accede to such a request. Notice I said "participating in the cat's care." Even if you get a cat because your child wants it, the final responsibility is yours to make sure that the cat is cared for appropriately.

Young children (six to nine years of age) need you to show and tell them—again and again—how much to feed, when to feed, and how and when to groom the cat. Preteens and teenagers are more capable of taking on such responsibilities, but they also have school, homework, jobs, and sports or other extracurricular activities in their lives. Your child may make all the promises in the world to feed the cat every day, brush him, and scoop the litter box, but you need to be willing and able to do those things when your child forgets to do them or even loses interest in the cat. Don't get a cat for your child unless you want one yourself.

HAPPY BIRTHDAY TO YOU

I want to get my daughter a cat for her birthday, which falls on Christmas day, but all the breeders and shelters I've talked to won't let me take a kitten home then. Why not?

The idea of presenting a child (or an adult) with the gift of a kitten on a birthday or at Christmas is irresistible. It is, however, a bad idea. First, you need to know that the individual actually wants and is committed to caring for a cat. Second, introducing a kitten to her new home should be done without a lot of fuss and fanfare. Birthday parties and holiday celebrations usually involve lots of screaming kids, wrapping paper, food, and other elements that can stress or cause harm to a kitten. Breeders and shelters know this and require that the kitten be brought into the home at a quieter time when the focus can be on her instead of on the festivities.

Rather than giving the actual kitten as a gift, present your daughter with a box or envelope that contains the kitten's picture, with a note stating what date she can be picked up. The box could also contain a collar and a cat toy to signify the coming gift.

CATS AND BABIES

We're having our first baby in a few months. Is now a good time to get a cat?

That depends in large part on whether you get a cat or a kitten. A kitten will be mischievous and lively for at least the first two years of his life. A new baby will require your full attention at all hours of the day and night for the first two years of his life. Dealing with a kitten and a new baby at the same time can be a bit much for even the most energetic and patient of people.

A mature cat, on the other hand, is less destructive and less active than a kitten. She's content to watch you while you care for the baby. On the rare occasions when you get a chance to sit down, you can relax by petting her while she purrs in your lap. Like kittens, adult cats need play and exercise, but a few minutes here and a few minutes there every day will satisfy them.

PURR THERAPY

I've been doing therapy work with my dog and enjoy it very much. Can cats be trained as therapy animals?

With their soft coats and rumbling purrs, many cats with a social nature do great work as animal therapists. Stroking a cat helps to reduce stress levels in people and can even lower their blood pressure. Therapists also use cats in different types of rehabilitation programs. For instance, petting a cat or holding a cat toy can help patients improve their mobility and upper-body strength, as well as learn impulse control and gentleness. Walking a cat on a leash under a therapist's supervision can improve lower-body strength. Feline therapists can help Alzheimer's patients dredge up long-forgotten memories of past pets, encourage people to talk, and increase self-esteem through their unconditional acceptance. In any therapy situation, cats are great conversation starters.

Cats suited to therapy work like people and are calm and relaxed around them, even in crowds. They often enjoy learning tricks and performing them for people, although this isn't a must. If your cat is a "Hail fellow, well met" type who likes to snuggle up to any and all visitors, he's a good candidate for therapy work. With lots of early socialization—exposure to all kinds of people, places, sounds, and experiences—you can help a kitten develop a therapeutic personality.

HOW SOON IS TOO SOON?

We had to euthanize our thirteen-year-old cat a couple of weeks ago. I miss her and want to get another cat, but my husband thinks it's too soon. How long should we wait?

There's no right answer to this question. Some people feel the need to fill that hole in their heart with another cat as soon as possible. For them, buying or adopting a new cat right away is the best decision. Others need time to mourn before they open their lives to another cat. Don't let anyone pressure you into making a decision that isn't right for your circumstances.

Not only is each situation unique, each cat is unique. When you acquire a new cat after your previous one has died, don't make the mistake of expecting her to be just like your previous cat. Even if they look alike, their temperaments and personalities may be very different. You might even want to consider getting a cat that's a different color or pattern from your previous cat, or a female if your other cat was male. It's unfair to burden a new cat with expectations she can never meet. Love her for her own self, and don't make comparisons.

ARE YOU SURE YOU'RE READY?

Things to consider before you get a cat are the time, expense, and lifetime commitment you'll be making. Ask yourself the following questions before you decide to share your life with a cat.

Why do I want a cat? The best reason for getting a cat is the desire for companionship. You should get a cat because you want one, not because your kids are nagging you for a pet. Unless you, too, would enjoy the presence of a cat in your home, tell your kids they'll have to wait until they're grown up to get a cat. Explain all the responsibilities and work involved so they'll understand your reasons, even if they disagree with it.

Do I have the time for a cat? Cats are easier to care for than dogs, but they still require an effort. They must be fed regularly, groomed, played with, and their litter box scooped. Expect to spend at least one to two hours a day caring for and interacting with your cat. (That's not counting the time you spend just watching television together or sleeping in the same room.)

Can I afford a cat? Adopting a cat from a shelter often costs $50 or more. The adoption fee usually covers a health exam and vaccinations and sometimes spay/neuter surgery. Purchasing a cat from a breeder can cost $200 and up. Having a cat spayed or neutered by your own veterinarian costs $100 to $150. To keep your cat healthy, you'll want to provide a high-quality cat food, at a cost of several hundred dollars per year. Cats need an annual visit to the veterinarian for a health exam, plus visits to the vet for any illnesses that come up. The cost of office visits varies regionally, but generally you can expect to pay $30 to

$40. Diagnostic tests such as fecal exams, blood panels, and X-rays or ultrasound exams can range from $20 to $200. If you go on vacation, you need to arrange for boarding or a pet sitter. Cats get hairballs (especially when they go ungroomed). You'll need stain remover for the carpet. Cat litter, a litter box, toys, a collar and tags, and other kitty paraphernalia cost money as well. The average cost of owning a cat for the first year can range from $700 to $1,000 or more.

Can I deal with the downside? I've said before that the relationship with a cat is like a marriage. Just as you and your spouse aren't perfect (if you are, I don't want to hear about it), no animal is perfect either. Your cat may have toilet accidents in the house, break something you treasure, or develop a health problem that's expensive to treat. When your cat gets old, she may get cranky and noisy in the middle of the night, frequently waking you from a sound sleep (I know this from experience).

Am I willing to make a lifetime commitment to this cat? To steal a catch phrase from the dog side, cats are for life, not just for Christmas. That cute, playful kitten or adult cat you fell in love with will be a cat with a mind of his own. Cats can live to be fifteen years or more. Some go on into their twenties. Will you still have room in your life for a cat five years from now? Ten years? A cat can be a burden you don't want to carry if you're in debt from student loans, are planning to have a child soon, or have a yen to see the world. Really think about your life plans as you consider whether a cat is right for you. If none of these warnings deter you, read on!

CHAPTER 2

Where to Find Your New Cat

WHEN YOU'RE READY to acquire a new cat, you have a number of options. You can purchase a pedigreed kitten from a breeder, adopt a kitten from a shelter, or adopt an adult cat from a shelter or breeder. Each alternative has advantages and disadvantages. Which you choose depends entirely on your situation, personality, and expectations. Don't let anyone pressure you into making a decision that isn't right for your circumstances.

Purchasing a pedigreed cat might be of interest if you want a cat with a specific look or personality. A pedigreed cat is also a good choice if you're interested in exhibiting at cat shows. Adopting a kitten or adult cat from a shelter is the thing to do if you simply want to enjoy life with a cat, any cat. Animal shelters house cats of all ages, coats, and colors. You're sure to find a cat that appeals to you there, and as a bonus, you're saving a life. What if you want a cat of a particular breed, but would rather not go through the trials of kittenhood? Consider adopting a retired show or breeding cat from a breeder or acquiring one through a breed-rescue organization.

Acquiring a cat from a breeder ensures that you get a cat of the breed, personality, color, or coat type that interests you. There are more than forty-five distinct cat breeds, and they come in a variety of colors, patterns, coat types, body types, and personalities. A pedigreed cat from a reputable breeder has been bred not only for a specific look, but also for health and temperament. You can meet the parents and sometimes the grandparents to ensure that they have good health and pleasant personalities.

An additional benefit of purchasing a cat from a breeder is his or her experience in evaluating the feline personality. A good breeder can help you choose the kitten or adult cat that's best suited to your lifestyle. She can steer you away from the active kitten whose sole goal in life is to climb Mount Everest and toward the laid-back kitten who'd rather play with a catnip mouse—or vice versa, depending on your needs. A responsible breeder will also inform you about her breed's personality and quirks. What may be charming to some can be downright disturbing to others. Abyssinians are active and inquisitive. Siamese like to "talk" all day long. Persians and Himalayans have a quiet, regal demeanor. Be sure you understand and will enjoy the personality of the pedigreed cat you choose.

The main disadvantage of purchasing a pedigreed cat is the expense. The cost of a pedigreed cat can range from a couple of hundred dollars to more than $1,000, depending on the cat's quality (a contender for the show ring versus a mismarked kitten suitable for pet life), the breed's rarity (popular breeds such as Persians and Siamese tend to be less expensive than, say, a Havana Brown or a Sphynx, which are not seen as commonly), and the breeder's location (generally, prices are higher on the East and West Coasts). No matter which breed you choose, if you want a cat you can show and breed from, expect to pay top dollar. On the other hand, there's no reason to pay $1,000 for a pet-quality cat, says Japanese Bobtail breeder Carolyn Vella of Blandon, Pennsylvania.

Depending on the breed you're interested in, you may find that another disadvantage to purchasing a pedigreed cat is the long wait for a kitten. For a rare breed, you may be put on a waiting list for kittens that won't be born for several months or even a year. Expect to pay a deposit, which may or may not be refundable, and to be placed on a waiting list.

If you know you want a pedigreed kitten and you've chosen a breed, the next step is to find a reputable breeder. How can you recognize reputable breeders? They are committed to improving the breed. They belong to cat clubs and exhibit cats of their breeding. They work to eliminate health problems by screening the cats in their breeding programs for genetic disease. They stay current on health-related issues, such as vaccinations, diseases, and genetics. They socialize their kittens so they'll be good companions. And they screen the buyers of their kittens to ensure that they go only to the best homes. Good breeders like to stay in touch with the buyers of their kittens and can be excellent resources if you run into behavior or health problems as your kitten matures.

To find a breeder, contact one of the cat registries for referrals. Cat registries include the Cat Fanciers Association (CFA), The International Cat Association (TICA), the American Cat Fanciers Association (ACFA), the American Association of Cat Enthusiasts (AACE), and the Canadian Cat Association (CCA). You might also ask your veterinarian or other cat owners for referrals. Magazines such as *Cat Fancy* and *Cats USA* are good sources of breeder advertisements.

Breeders can also be found at cat shows. Attend a cat show and talk to breeders there. Look for knowledgeable breeders who are interested in talking about their breeds and are willing to take the time to educate a novice. If you meet a breeder you like at a show, make an appointment to see her cats in their home setting. Without examining the cattery, it's difficult to know how the kitten has been socialized or in what conditions he has been raised.

If you're interested in acquiring an adult cat of a particular breed, or the cost of a pedigreed kitten is beyond your means, consider adopting a cat through a breed rescue group. Sometimes, through no fault of their own, pedigreed cats find themselves homeless, and that's when breed-rescue groups step in. Often sponsored by national, regional, or local breed clubs, these organizations take in and place pedigreed cats that have lost their homes through an owner's death or divorce, or because they were in an unhealthy environment. Breed-rescue groups provide temporary housing, evaluate the cats' personalities and health, provide health care such as vaccinations or spay/neuter surgery if needed, and then screen potential adopters to find the best home for a given cat. Breed-rescue groups are available for most cat breeds. To find them, contact the national cat registries such as CFA or TICA, or check their Web sites for more information. Adoptable cats aren't always available, but you can place your name on a waiting list until the right one comes along.

Another good way to acquire an adult pedigreed cat is to adopt a retired breeding or show cat. Many breeders like to place these retired cats in pet homes so they can have the attention from a family that a busy breeder/exhibitor might not have time to give. (She's not a cat, but that's how we acquired Bella, our first Cavalier King Charles Spaniel, and we have rejoiced in our good fortune every day since.)

What if you simply want a good old domestic shorthair (or longhair)? There are plenty of those to go around, and they can be a wonderful choice, especially for the first-time cat owner. You can find a nice kitten or cat of just about every color, coat type, or temperament at your local animal shelter. You might even find a cat that resembles a Siamese, Persian, or other pedigreed cat, although he won't come with papers, of course. Adopting a cat from an animal shelter brings the satisfaction of having a one-of-a-kind cat, as well as knowing that you've saved a life.

You may hesitate to adopt an adult cat from a shelter, fearing that he will come with health or behavior problems. Fortunately, that's rarely the case. Many cats end up in shelters because their owners are irresponsible, not because of anything the cat did wrong. That's not to say that a cat adopted from a shelter can't or won't have a behavioral or health problem, but chances are good that you'll end up with a nice cat that will be a wonderful companion.

Knowing what to look for in a shelter and in a cat can help you make the right decision. When we think of the animal shelter, the picture that usually comes to mind is a municipal animal shelter, known as "the pound" in the old days. Today, modern municipal shelters enforce animal control ordinances, license animals, quarantine animals that have bitten someone, and identify stray animals and return them to their families when possible. Progressive municipal shelters with adequate budgets may offer such services as animal placement, community education, and vaccination clinics.

Your town may also have one or more privately funded nonprofit animal shelters. Private shelters with open admissions take any cat brought to them. So-called no-kill shelters pick and choose which cats they'll accept, based on age, health, adoptability, and availability of kennel space. Once they accept an animal, it has a home there until it's adopted, no matter how long that may take. Whether municipal or private, no two animal shelters are alike, and there is no such thing as a centrally organized SPCA or humane society that oversees local organizations.

The greatest advantage of adopting a cat from a shelter is that warm, fuzzy feeling you get from giving a good home to a cat in need. Another advantage is the variety of services provided by some shelters. You may go home with a cat that has been health-checked, spayed or neutered, and vaccinated. Some shelters offer counseling to help you choose the cat that's right for your lifestyle. Shelter personnel see the cats on a daily basis and can give you insight into each cat's personality and habits. Often, shelter cats come with background information, such as whether they get along with dogs or children, or if they prefer men or women. If a cat was turned in by his owners, the shelter is likely to have more detailed information about his health, habits, and personality than about a cat found as a stray.

Ideally, the home situation you can offer will be similar to what the cat is already accustomed to. For instance, old cats may have a difficult time fitting in to a home with very young children unless they came from a family with children. On the other hand, most outdoor cats adjust well to becoming indoor cats.

Like breeders and breed-rescue groups, certain shelters don't provide instant gratification. They often put potential adopters through a rigorous screening process before letting them take a cat home. While it might seem onerous, think of it as a benefit to the cat rather than as a hoop you must jump through.

If the only place available for you to adopt a cat is an understaffed, overburdened city shelter, ask an experienced cat owner to go with you and guide your decision. It's one thing to take home a cat with an unknown history that has been evaluated by a trained shelter employee. It's quite another to take home an animal without knowing anything at all about him. An experienced person can help you determine what the cat knows, where he needs help, and how to work with him to bring out his inner good cat. Nonetheless, whatever risk there may be in adopting a cat with an unknown past can usually be overcome by working with the shelter, your veterinarian, or a behaviorist after the adoption.

There's no right or wrong choice when it comes to deciding whether to purchase a cat from a breeder or adopt one from a shelter or rescue organization. Consider all the factors that are important to you—color or pattern, coat type, breed or mix, temperament, competition in cat shows—and then make the decision that feels right. Following is some more information to help you find the cat that's right for you.

TOP TEN KITTY HIT PARADE

What are the most popular cat breeds?

The Cat Fanciers Association is the world's largest registry of pedigreed cats. According to the CFA's registration statistics, the top ten cat breeds are the Persian, Maine Coon, Siamese, Exotic Shorthair, Abyssinian, Oriental, Birman, Scottish Fold, American Shorthair, and Burmese.

PURCHASING A PEDIGREED CAT

How can I know if the breeder I'm interviewing is reputable? What questions should I ask?

Good question! A reputable breeder has a strong interest in finding out about your lifestyle and experience with cats so she can make sure you will provide a happy home for one of her kittens. Not only does she want her kitten to be happy with you, she wants you to be happy with her kitten. Look for someone who enjoys talking about her breed and is willing to take the time to educate a novice.

Start your conversation by asking about the breed's personality and temperament and grooming requirements. Ask if any genetic problems affect the breed and what steps the breeder takes to screen for and eliminate those problems. Let the breeder know what you're looking for in a cat—quiet, active, talkative, easy to groom—so she can tell you if her breed is appropriate.

Other questions to ask:

- What's the goal of your breeding program?
- How long have you been breeding cats?
- How frequently do you have litters?
- Do you participate in a cattery inspection program?
- Do your kittens come with a health guarantee or a veterinary health certificate?
- What are the health problems in this breed?
- Were the kittens' parents screened for those health problems?
- Can you show me proof and results of those tests?
- Do you belong to a national cat association and subscribe to its code of ethics?
- Do you exhibit your cats?
- Do you provide a pedigree and registration papers for your kittens?
- Can you give me references from other buyers of your kittens?

A reputable breeder will welcome your interest and won't be offended by any of these questions. She's happy to show you where she raises her kittens and explain her breeding program and the steps she takes to produce healthy, well-socialized cats. (See the Test Scores section later in this chapter to learn more about the genetic diseases that can affect cats.) She doesn't breed more than two or three litters a year—more than that and she would have too many cats to give them all the individual attention they need. Breeders who belong to national cat associations and who exhibit their cats indicate a desire to improve the breed. They're proud of what they produce and are willing for the cats to be judged by other fanciers.

When you visit a breeder's home, use your eyes, nose, and common sense, says Maine Coon breeder Lynn Hofstetter. "No home should look tattered. I have a houseful of cats and I have leather furniture, a baby grand piano, and upholstered furniture in the den, along with three scratching posts that the cats and kittens use. No home should smell of urine, and no kitten should appear nappy looking, dirty, or ill. I have many litter boxes and scoop three times a day. If the kittens are off in a corner and won't interact at all or can't be handled, think twice about taking one home. You want a kitten who will be a wonderful companion for sixteen or more years."

The great thing about purchasing a kitten from a reputable breeder is that he or she will always be available as a resource to you, throughout your cat's life. Good breeders are delighted to be able to follow their kittens as they grow up and help with questions about behavior and health.

A pedigreed cat has a specific look and personality, but he may also have special needs, such as daily grooming

WHITE GLOVE INSPECTION

What's a cattery inspection program? I didn't know there was such a thing.

Several cat organizations, including CFA, TICA, ACFA, and AACE, offer cattery inspection programs. The breeder pays for the inspection, which is performed by a licensed veterinarian. Each program operates in a similar manner, with some minor differences.

Generally, catteries are evaluated for such factors as cage size, cleanliness, state of repair, ventilation, lighting, and overall appearance. The veterinarian notes whether litter boxes are clean; rates adequacy of food, water, bedding, and exercise space; and observes whether there's an isolation area for sick cats, show cats, and newborns. The breeder must exhibit good record keeping, including proof of vaccinations and appropriate parasite prevention, and provide proper storage of medications and vaccines. In addition, the veterinarian rates the condition of the cats and the socialization of the kittens. A high rating isn't a guarantee that your kitten will be perfect, but it is evidence of a breeder's commitment to high standards.

THE THIRD DEGREE

The breeders I've talked to ask an awful lot of questions. Some of them seem pretty intrusive. The rescue groups and animal shelters are the same way. Some of them even require home visits before they'll sell or adopt out a cat. Don't they want to place their cats?

Reputable breeders and concerned breed-rescue groups and animal shelters want the very best for the kittens and cats in their care. It's important to them that their cats go to homes where they will be loved and cared for the rest of their lives. No breeder wants her kittens to lose their home someday because she selected the wrong family for them. In fact, many reputable breeders make it a condition of sale that if there's ever a reason you can't keep the cat you purchased from them, you must return him rather than give him away or place him in a shelter.

Breed-rescue groups and animal shelters have the same concerns. They know it's not good for a cat's emotional health to return to a shelter again and again. They want to place him in the right home the first time.

Expect a breeder or shelter worker to ask some or all of the following questions:

- Why do you want a cat? Be prepared to explain why you (and other family members) would enjoy the company of a cat and what you expect from a relationship with a cat.
- Why are you interested in this breed? Use this question as an opportunity to show that you've done your homework on the breed. You should have some idea about personality and grooming needs, for instance.
- If you have cats now, are they spayed or neutered? Besides preventing unwanted kittens, spaying and neutering offer health and behavior benefits for cats (see chapter seven). Shelters that ask this question want to ensure that you are a responsible owner who won't be producing more kittens for them to place. Breeders want to ensure that you're a responsible owner who won't breed a cat just for the "fun" or "education" of the experience. Reputable breeders breed only cats that have been health tested and that are good examples of their breed, both physically and temperamentally.
- Do you keep your cats indoors? Indoor cats lead safer, longer, healthier lives. They are better protected from disease and injury than cats allowed to roam freely outdoors. Breeders and shelter staff want to know if you care enough to keep your cat safe inside.
- How many other cats/dogs/kids do you have? It's fine if you have other animals or children. (The only exception might be if

you have an extremely large number of other pets, and then there may be concern that the new cat will get lost in the shuffle.) Give an idea of how your other pets (and children, if applicable) interact with each other—do they get along in general, how do the dogs feel about cats, do the dogs have a high prey drive that might endanger the kitten, are the children old enough to interact gently with a kitten?

- Does anyone in your family have allergies? Many cats end up in shelters because family members have or develop allergies. You need to explain how you would handle the situation if allergies are or become an issue. Are you willing to help keep the cat with the family by making adjustments such as bathing the cat more frequently, using dander-reducing sprays, vacuuming more frequently, or keeping the cat out of the allergic person's bedroom?

- How long did your previous pets live and why did they die? Ideally, of course, your other pets lived long, healthy lives and died of old age. If your previous cat was hit by a car or suffered some other accident, explain how you'd prevent such an occurrence from happening again.

- Is anyone home during the day? Cats do well on their own, so it's not a must for someone to be home during the day, although it's a plus. If you work sixteen hours a day and then come home and sleep, though, you might want to reconsider getting any pet at all.

- Do you own your home? Be prepared to prove that you own your home or that your landlord permits pets. Too many people try to sneak cats into rentals or give their cats up when they move because they don't put enough effort into finding a place that allows pets. No breeder or shelter wants to send a cat into an uncertain situation.

- Do you have a veterinarian or can you provide references from your veterinarian? If this is your very first pet, you may not have a veterinarian yet (see chapter seven on how to find a veterinarian). If you do, it's a plus if your vet is willing to testify to your good pet-care skills.

Don't be insulted when a breeder or animal shelter employee gives you the third degree. Count yourself lucky that you've found someone who cares enough to make sure you and the cat are right for each other. Someone who seems in too much of a hurry to let you have one of her kittens or who isn't interested in your background may not be someone you want to deal with.

RED FLAGS

Are there any warning signs that a breeder isn't all she should be?

The breeder who's churning out kittens just for the money is likely to tell you not to worry about health testing—his cats never have any problems. Run the other direction if you hear a breeder make such a claim without being able to back it up.

Other red flags include lack of a sales contract or health guarantee, no interest in exhibiting his cats, no membership in a national cat organization, and a willingness to let kittens go before they are twelve weeks old. At twelve weeks, kittens have had their basic inoculations and have developed the physical and social stability needed to adapt to a new environment.

Be wary of someone who tries to push a cat on you, and insist on seeing the cattery or at least the breeder's home. "If the cattery or house is dirty or smells, don't even think about buying a kitten from that person," Vella says. "If you see cats running around but they're shy, walk away. The kittens aren't being socialized. The cats should want to play with you and be curious about you. That's generally a sign of a pretty good environment."

LONG-DISTANCE RELATIONSHIP

I've found a breeder I like, but she's not in my area. Is it a good idea to purchase a kitten long-distance?

It's not always possible to find the perfect breeder living right next door, or even in the same town. Sometimes you have to look a little farther afield for the kitten of your dreams, especially if you're interested in one of the more unusual cat breeds. Buying a pedigreed kitten sight unseen may seem as if you're asking for trouble, but it can be done successfully.

Expect to spend lots of time on the phone or communicating via e-mail with the breeder so the two of you can get to know each other. It's not unusual for a phone interview to go on for an hour or two, or to have several phone conversations for briefer periods over several days or weeks. It's important for you and the breeder to be comfortable with each other.

Check out each other's references. She may be able to refer you to someone in your area who has bought one of her kittens. She may have a friend in your town who can visit your home and report back to her on the environment you'd provide for one of her kittens. And you may have a relative in the breeder's hometown who can give a thumbs-up to the state of the breeder's cattery and kittens.

The postal service and the Internet are your friends as well. The breeder can send photos or videos of her cats and kittens, or direct you to her Web site. Ask for copies of health certifications, just as you would if you were meeting the breeder in person.

Assuming you come to an agreement on the purchase of a kitten, the next step is getting it. Some breeders will ship their kittens, while others prefer that they be delivered in person. Breeders who do ship their kittens will be familiar with the regulations involved and will choose the flight that will be fastest and safest for the kitten. Better and safer than shipping is having the kitten hand-carried by someone in the airline cabin. You or the breeder may know someone who's headed in your direction and would be willing to take the kitten on board (in her carrier, of course) and deliver her to you at the airport. The agreement with the breeder should include a forty-eight-hour no-questions-asked return policy, so make the veterinarian's office your first stop after the airport pickup. You want to make sure the kitten is healthy and in good condition. Avoid breeders who sell only on a "no returns allowed" basis. If all is well, take the kitten home, let the breeder know she arrived safely, and start enjoying life with your new cat.

SHOW SALE

Can I purchase a cat at a cat show?

The answer is a qualified yes. Some breeders may have kittens or adult cats available for sale at shows. A cat bought at a show shouldn't be an impulse buy, however. You should already have interviewed the breeder, seen her adult cats in their home environment, and be familiar with the breed and its needs. Of course, the kitten or cat you purchase should be friendly and healthy, with clean ears, eyes, and nose (no runny discharge from any of these orifices), a shiny coat, and no sign of respiratory problems such as coughing or sneezing.

MEETING BREEDERS

I know you said a cat show is a good place to find breeders, but none of them seem interested in talking to me. Am I doing something wrong?

It could be that your timing is off. Breeders preparing cats for exhibition are busy with the final grooming touches to ensure that their cats look perfect, not to mention calming their own nerves. If you find a breeder you're interested in talking to further, ask when would be a good time to come back. The breeder will appreciate your consideration and will be relaxed and ready to chat when you return. You can also take her business card and call her after the show if that's more convenient.

FINDING LOVE IN THE CLASSIFIEDS

I saw a classified ad for a cat that seems perfect. Is it okay to buy a cat through the newspaper?

Buying a cat through the classifieds can work out as long as you do your homework. You'll find that most reputable breeders don't advertise in the newspaper because they usually have waiting lists for their kittens or prefer to advertise in cat magazines. However, you might find a classified ad for an adult pedigreed cat that a breeder wants to place in a pet home. Interview the breeder just as thoroughly as you would if you were purchasing a kitten. Find out why he wants to place the cat (good reasons being that the cat is retired from the show ring or retired from breeding and he wants her to enjoy life as a pet where she can get lots of human attention). Breeders often feel that they are too busy with kittens or show cats to give retirees the attention they deserve. Be sure to meet the cat in her home environment, where she's comfortable, so you can get a true picture of her personality.

You will also find that many animal shelters and cat rescue organizations advertise prospective pets in the classifieds. Ads often specify the cat's color, coat type, and personality ("loves kids" or "hates dogs" or "wants to be an only cat"). This can be a good way for you to screen cats in advance before you go to meet them. To be sure it's really a rescue, look for an identifying name, such as Stanford Cat Network or Persian and Himalayan Cat Rescue. The same advice applies to cats advertised on bulletin boards at pet supply stores or veterinary offices.

THAT KITTY IN THE WINDOW

There are so many cute kittens at the pet store in the mall. It would be a lot easier to just get one there than to spend all that time finding and interviewing a breeder. Is there any reason I shouldn't buy a cat at the pet store?

There are two answers to this question, depending on the pet store. Pet stores that sell kittens usually acquire them from commercial breeders, sometimes referred to as kitten mills. Commercial breeders produce cats on a large scale and don't have the time to give them the human attention they need at a young age to become properly socialized. Their breeding cats (and the kittens they produce) often live in small cages their entire lives (or until they're shipped to the pet store) rather than being raised in a home environment where they can get plenty of human touch and interaction. Nor do commercial breeders perform health testing to screen breeding stock for genetic diseases. They also ship kittens to pet stores at an early age, so they don't get as much time with their mother and littermates, learning how to be good cats. And kittens that have been shipped long distances can become stressed and more prone to illness. Some pet stores sell locally acquired kittens as young as four weeks of age, which is far too early for them to be weaned and away from their mother. They are likely to grow up to have behavior problems because they haven't had the training from mother and socialization from humans that teaches them how to be cats and live successfully with people.

Other drawbacks to pet store kittens are that you can't meet the parents and you don't know what kind of environment they were raised in. You don't get registration papers, and sometimes you don't even get the breed you thought you were buying. "With a breeder, you know what you're getting," says Vella. "For instance, Devon Rex kittens molt; they literally lose all their hair. There have been Devon Rex sold as Sphynx. Then the hair comes back and the person discovers that he has a Rex."

Even if a pet store claims that it acquires kittens from local breeders, keep in mind that no reputable breeder would permit her kittens to be sold in such a way. Remember, reputable breeders screen their kitten buyers to ensure that they'll provide good lifetime homes. Pet store kittens are usually purchased on impulse rather than as a result of thought and research.

That said, some pet supply stores permit shelters or rescue groups to display kittens available for adoption. This is a great way to see a small selection of kittens or cats, rather than being overwhelmed by the numbers you'll find at a shelter facility. You must still be screened by the adoption group before taking your kitten home, but it's more convenient than going to the shelter. Choose to support this type of pet store rather than the ones that sell kittens for profit. If you want a pedigreed cat, you'll get more for your money from a reputable breeder (screening of parents, health guarantee, home socialization). If you simply want a nice cat, you'll do more good by adopting one from a pet supply store that supports animal shelters than by purchasing one from a pet store that supports commercial breeders.

DOLLAR SIGNS

Why do pedigreed cats cost so much?

Breeding cats is an expensive hobby. Few breeders find that it is a money-making business. First, of course, there's the process of acquiring breeding stock. A show-quality or breeding-quality pedigreed cat's price can start at $500 and go up to $1,800 or more. Multiply that by however many cats the breeder has in her breeding program, and the amount comes to a pretty chunk of change.

Depending on the size of the cattery, food and litter costs can be $250 per month and up. Just like the rest of us, breeders must purchase cat carriers, scratching posts, food and water bowls, litter boxes, grooming equipment, and medication. Customized cattery setups can cost $5,000 or more. There are veterinary bills for normal expenses such as annual exams and vaccinations, as well as for the costs of health screening, kitten exams, and unexpected illnesses or injuries. For all of these expenses, breeders can spend $500 or more per cat per year.

Reputable breeders show their cats. Entry fees for shows add up. Showing a cat to the title of champion can cost $500 to $2,000. Showing a cat to the title of grand champion or regional/national winner can cost an additional $1,000, an amount that can rise to an astounding $20,000. Peripheral costs of showing cats include hotel stays, gas for and wear and tear on the car, and meals for the weekend.

Then there are stud fees if someone else's male is used in a breeding. Stud fees of $500 to $1,000 aren't unusual. If the stud is out of town, the breeder must pay to take or ship the female to him.

When a litter is born, the mother may need a Caesarean section in case of an emergency. That can cost $750 or more. Veterinary care until the kittens are placed at three to four months of age is about $100 per kitten—assuming none of them have any health problems. The breeder also spends a lot of time caring for, socializing, and cleaning up after the kittens. If the mother dies in labor or rejects the kittens, they must be hand-fed round the clock until they can eat solid food.

As you can see, reputable breeders have a lot invested in their kittens. The amount they charge usually barely covers their costs. When you think about it, you're getting a bargain: a healthy, well-socialized kitten with a distinctive look and personality. You get far more for your money when you buy from a reputable breeder than you do when you buy from a pet store or a breeder who cuts corners. Wouldn't you rather spend your money on a cat that has a head start in life through his parents' good health and qualities as well as his own good diet, vaccinations, deworming, and early socialization than on one raised without any thought as to how he will eventually turn out?

FREE TO A GOOD HOME

My neighbor's Siamese cat had kittens and she's giving them away for free. I really love Siamese cats, and getting a kitten from my neighbor would be easier and a lot less expensive than buying one from a breeder. Is this a good idea?

The first cat I acquired as an adult was a Siamese mix from a "free to a good home" ad. I should have thought a little more carefully about taking her home when the guy who answered the door told me that if I could catch her I could have her. Trouble wasn't very well socialized, but I was lucky and she settled nicely into my apartment, although she hid under the bed for the first three days as well as whenever anyone else came over.

I'm guessing that this was an unplanned pregnancy (one reason that spaying is so important) and that your neighbor doesn't know or only suspects who the father is. If that's the case, there are some "ifs" to be considered here. If you like your neighbor's cat's personality, if your neighbor's cat has a record of good health, if your neighbor is raising the kittens in her home and giving them lots of socialization, and if you don't mind that your kitten doesn't come with registration papers or parents with health screening, this may be a good way for you to acquire a kitten.

Take a pass on kittens being offered free at, say, the grocery store. You have no way of knowing the parents' temperaments or health or how the kittens have been raised and socialized.

Keep in mind, too, that there's really no such thing as a free kitten. You'll spend at least $200 acquiring all the paraphernalia a kitten needs: food, litter box, veterinary exam, spay/neuter surgery, toys, food dishes, and so on. Another thing to remember is that you get what you pay for: A kitten from a reputable breeder might cost more, but you'll usually receive a health guarantee, plus you have the breeder as a resource in case you run into health or behavior problems.

BUYING VERSUS ADOPTING

I know that there are more cats than there are homes for all of them. If I buy a cat from a breeder, am I contributing to this feline population explosion? Wouldn't it be better for me to adopt one that really needs a home?

There's nothing wrong with wanting a pedigreed cat. We all have likes and desires and preferences when it comes to animal companions, and it's perfectly acceptable to purchase a cat from a reputable breeder if she has what you're looking for. Irresponsible breeders who don't screen their kittens' buyers are the ones who contribute to the pet overpopulation problem.

There's no doubt, however, that you do a lot of good when you adopt a cat from a shelter or rescue group. What's most important, however, is for you to be satisfied with your new cat. If you've always wanted a Maine Coon, by all means, seek out a good breeder or a rescue group and get one.

ADOPTING OVER THE INTERNET

When you can't find the cat you want at a local shelter, it's time to take to the highway—the Internet highway, that is. A Web site called petfinder.com plays matchmaker for people and pets nationwide. Janine Adams of St. Louis, Missouri, found her first cat, Joe, indirectly through Petfinder.

"We had decided that we were ready for a cat, and my husband, Barry, wanted a gray one. At the suggestion of a dog-trainer friend, I contacted a rescuer, who told me via e-mail about a gray cat she had available and gave me the URL to look her up on Petfinder. I must have looked at her picture a dozen times; it was great to have something to refer to as I waited for the day of our meeting. I made arrangements to meet that cat with Pip, my standard Poodle," she says. "As it turned out, the foster mom thought Pip would be too overwhelming for this particular cat, but she had another cat at home, an orange one, that loved dogs. She brought Joe over, and the rest is history."

Simply log on at www.petfinder.com and enter your search requirements. Rescue groups and shelter workers post descriptions and sometimes photos of cats who need homes. You can search by breed, age, gender, and locale. Once you find an animal that meets your requirements, you can contact the rescue group or shelter directly. You can also find a cat through your local shelter's Web site.

Just as you would with any adoption, ask questions, be patient, and trust your instincts. Avoid sites that offer animals for auction (it's against the rules on eBay, for instance). And if you're looking at a breeder's Web site, remember that a clever Web designer can make anyone look good. Ask the same tough questions you would of someone you met at a cat show.

TEST SCORES

Reputable breeders check their cats for contagious and heritable diseases before breeding them. Any cat can acquire the feline leukemia virus (FeLV) or feline immunodeficiency virus (FIV). A good cattery is free of both of these fatal diseases because the breeder has his cats tested regularly for them.

Breeders should also have their cats blood-typed before breeding them, Vella says. When the parents' blood types are incompatible, it can cause fading kitten syndrome. Kittens will seem to be fine for a while but then go downhill suddenly and die. A breeder who doesn't perform blood-typing before breeding his cats or who isn't even aware of it probably isn't someone you want to buy from.

Some breeds are prone to genetic diseases, which can be passed on from parents to kittens. Know what diseases may affect the breed you're interested in, and ask the breeder for copies of the parents' test results. For instance, a Maine Coon breeder should be able to show that her breeding cats' hips are certified good or excellent by the Orthopedic Foundation for Animals or the University of Pennsylvania's PennHIP program.

Some of the congenital (present at birth) and hereditary (passed from parents to offspring) diseases that can affect pedigreed cats are listed below. Some of these conditions can be corrected surgically, while others are fatal. Be aware as well that not all genetic diseases have tests yet and that some show up later in life.

Abyssinian: amyloidosis (a kidney disease); patellar luxation (dislocated kneecap)

Balinese: congenital heart defects; strabismus (crossed eyes); nystagmus (jerking eye movements)

Bengal: entropion (eyelid rolled inward)

Birman: congenital cataracts

Chartreux: patellar luxation (dislocated kneecap)

Cornish Rex: hypertrichosis (hereditary baldness)

Devon Rex: hypertrichosis (hereditary baldness); patellar luxation (dislocated kneecap); sensitivity to sun exposure

Exotic Shorthair: cherry eye; constricted nostrils; dental malocclusions (incorrect bites, such as an overbite or underbite); excessive tearing; seborrhea oleosa (scaly, greasy skin)

Himalayan: cherry eye; congenital cataracts; constricted nostrils; dental malocclusions (incorrect bites, such as an overbite or underbite); excessive tearing; polycystic kidney disease; portosystemic shunt (liver disease); seborrhea oleosa (scaly, greasy skin)

Javanese: congenital heart defects; strabismus (crossed eyes); nystagmus (jerking eye movements)

Korat: GM1 and GM2 gangliosidosis (lethal gene defects that cause fatal progressive brain disease)

Maine Coon: hip dysplasia (hip joint defect); hypertrophic cardiomyopathy (enlarged heart wall)

Manx: spina bifida (neurologic disorder); defecation problems

Norwegian Forest Cat: glycogen storage disease (an inherited abnormality of glucose metabolism)

Oriental: congenital heart defects; strabismus (crossed eyes); nystagmus (jerking eye movements)

Persian: cherry eye; congenital cataracts; congenital heart defects; constricted nostrils; dental malocclusions (incorrect bites, such as an overbite or underbite); entropion (eyelid rolled inward); excessive tearing; polycystic kidney disease; portosystemic shunt (liver disease); seborrhea oleosa (scaly, greasy skin)

Siamese: congenital heart defects; strabismus (crossed eyes); nystagmus (jerking eye movements); portosystemic shunt (liver disease); spina bifida (neurologic disorder)

Somali: autoimmune hemolytic disorder (premature destruction of red blood cells by immune system)

Sphynx: sensitivity to sun exposure

Turkish Angora: partial or total deafness in white cats with blue eyes

CHAPTER 3

What You Should Look for in Your New Cat

YOU'VE FINALLY DECIDED that you're ready for a cat, and have made the choice between a pedigreed pussycat or a shelter sweetie. Now you just need to choose the cat that's right for you. All kittens are cute, especially when four or five of them are rubbing up against your leg and mewing. If you're at a shelter, you may simply be overwhelmed by the numbers. Factors to consider include age, personality, condition, and breed.

Once you've made your decision, you'll need to be prepared to deal with sales and adoption contracts. Before we get into specifics, here are some things to look for when choosing your new kitten or cat.

Healthy animals have clear, bright eyes. A cat with runny eyes may have an infection or some other eye problem. Infections can be treated, of course, but as a first-time owner you're better off taking home a healthy cat.

Ears should be clean as well. Healthy ears are pink inside, with no bad smell. A cat with a crumbly brown discharge in his ears may have ear mites, which are highly contagious to other cats and dogs (but not to people). Cats that frequently shake their heads or scratch at their ears may have an ear infection or ear mites.

Coat and skin condition are also indicators of health. Look for a kitten or cat with a nice, full, shiny coat. A patchy or scabby coat suggests fleas or some kind of skin infection or disease.

Cats are prone to respiratory infections. Be concerned if a cat is sneezing, coughing, or has runny eyes.

Finally, the cat you choose should have an outgoing, confident but not aggressive temperament. Look for a kitten that likes to be petted, but avoid one that bites or scratches at you. The kitten that's hiding in a corner may seem vulnerable and appealing, but she may have emotional problems that are difficult if not impossible to overcome without a great deal of time and patience.

That said, you may want to allow some leeway if you're choosing a cat or kitten from a shelter. A shelter is stressful despite the caring staff, and the cats there may have some minor conditions that can be cleared up with a course of antibiotics or a bath and flea treatment. Take the cat to your veterinarian within forty-eight hours of the adoption or purchase to make sure he doesn't have any insurmountable health problems.

YOUTH VERSUS AGE

Kittens look like a lot of fun, but I'm not sure I have enough time to spend with one. Are there advantages to getting an adult cat?

Everybody loves a kitten. They're just so darned cute. On the downside, they need attention and training so they don't climb the curtains, claw the furniture, and otherwise wreak havoc. It can be exhausting to keep up with a kitten—hauling him down from the Christmas tree, sweeping up the fragments of broken figurines, being awakened at 2 a.m. by a tiny fuzzball bouncing on your head. Kittens have a seemingly endless supply of energy, and they may not settle into sedate cathood until they're two or three or even four years old.

Kittenhood has its pleasures, no doubt, but if a peaceful, gentle pet is what you're looking for, skip over the two or three years that kittenhood can last and go right for an adult cat. There are distinct advantages to choosing an adult cat. For one thing, you know what kind of personality you're getting. You may prefer an aloof cat that regards you as a can opener on legs to one that sits on your keyboard and pats your face while you're trying to type. Choosing an older cat can help ensure that you get exactly the personality you're looking for.

An older cat may already be neutered and vaccinated. Some adult cats in shelters are declawed, which may be a consideration if you're concerned about your furniture. (See chapter twelve for more about the controversial practice of declawing.)

Adult cats are more predictable. Because their personalities have already formed, you can better judge how they will fit into your household and how they will get along with your children or other pets. They may already have experience with dogs or kids, which can be a plus.

You may think that a kitten will be a better choice if you have children. Not necessarily. An older cat with family experience likely has more patience with children. Often the best type of cat for a young child is a large, neutered male who's two or three years old. This type of cat is usually mellow, tolerant, less likely to scratch and nip during play, and sturdier than a kitten, which can be easily injured. He's calm enough that a lot of commotion and the sudden moves of a child won't cause him to swish his tail and lash out with a claw.

If you have children, adult cats are simply less work than a kitten. They're content to snooze their time away while you're at work or to sit in your lap when you finally have a chance to rest from the day's exertions.

THE BATTLE OF THE SEXES

Should I get a boy or a girl? Does it matter?

Both male and female cats can have wonderful, sweet, loving person-alities. It all depends on the individual cat, although in my experience males tend to be more loving. There are other considerations related to gender, however.

Male cats that aren't neutered will get into fights if they're al-lowed outdoors. Inside, they'll mark their territory by spraying urine on walls, curtains, and furniture. Unspayed females will also mark territory by spraying, and they'll drive you crazy with their yowling demands for male attention every time they go into estrus, or heat, which occurs two or more times a year. Cats that are spayed or neutered no longer have the instinctive desire to reproduce, making them less likely to roam and fight.

Gender does have a one-time effect on your pocketbook. Neuter-ing is generally less expensive than spaying. Other than that consid-eration, your best bet is to choose a cat based on personality first, gender second.

PET QUALITY VERSUS SHOW QUALITY

The breeder says I should get a pet-quality kitten since I don't plan to show or breed him. Am I getting a second-rate kitten? If I'm spending a lot of money, I want the best.

Of course you want a good kitten, but don't turn up your nose at one that's labeled pet quality. That simply means that for whatever rea-son, the kitten isn't suitable for show or breeding purposes. He might not have the right markings or his eyes might not be the right color.

In Birmans, for instance, the main factor that separates pet- and show-quality kittens is the "gloving" on their feet, which must be even across the toes of all four feet, with little inverted V-shaped laces up the back legs. Pet-quality Birman kittens might have gloves or laces that are uneven. Other factors include color, size, symmetry, coat length, and whiteness of coat.

A pet-quality Bengal kitten might have ticking in the coat, giving it an uneven or unclear appearance. Rib stripes—black or dark brown bars or stripes in the pattern of spotting near the ribs—can also place a Bengal kitten in the pet-quality category. In the Siamese, the tail might be too short or have a slight kink. A white spot on the chest or ears or eyes that are just a tad too close or too far apart can make a kitten unsuited to the show ring. Sometimes there's nothing really wrong with the kitten's appearance; the breeder simply prefers a different look.

Every breed has different factors that distinguish pet-quality and show-quality kittens. The breeder should be able to show you the differences between the two. A pet-quality kitten might not be perfect in some of these cosmetic areas, but he will still have a great personality and good health. Those are the most important things for a cat who will be a companion.

THE PERFECT MATCH

Do different cat breeds have different personalities?

Yes, indeed. While cats don't vary quite as much in temperament and personality as dogs, they are highly individual and vary in temperament from breed to breed and individual to individual. Besides breed, other factors that can affect a cat's personality include early experiences and environment, the amount of socialization received during kittenhood, and the parents' personalities.

Some cats have quiet, calm personalities. If this appeals to you, consider such breeds as American, British or Exotic Shorthairs, Birmans,

Himalayans or Persians, and Ragdolls. Many nonpedigreed domestic shorthairs and longhairs also have this type of personality.

Lap cats enjoy lots of physical contact with their owners. They love sitting in a lap and being petted for hours on end. Cat breeds that often fall into this category include the American Curl; the American Shorthair; the Bombay; the British Shorthair; the Burmese; the Chartreux; the Cornish Rex and the Devon Rex; the Havana Brown; the Japanese Bobtail; the La Perm (named for his curly coat); the Manx and his long-coated cousin the Cymric; the Persian, Exotic Shorthair, and Himalayan; the Siamese, Balinese, Javanese, and Oriental; the Singapura; the Snowshoe; the Sphynx; the Tonkinese; and the York Chocolate.

More adventuresome, inquisitive breeds include the Abyssinian and his fluffier cousin the Somali; the Bengal; the Cornish Rex and Devon Rex; the Egyptian Mau; the Japanese Bobtail; the Ocicat; the Russian Blue; the Siamese, Balinese, Javanese, or Tonkinese; the Singapura; and the Turkish Angora or the Turkish Van.

Other cats fall somewhere in the middle. A domestic shorthair or longhair might fit into this moderate category, or he can have the calm, lap-loving, or active characteristics of the breeds described above. It's all in the genes.

CATS AND KIDS

Are some cat breeds better with children than others?

Generally, personality is the main consideration, but some breeds do have a reputation for being good with kids. They tend to be particularly easygoing and tolerant of being carried around or dressed up in doll clothes. Others are unusually energetic or trainable. Many breeds fall into the good-with-kids category, including the American Curl, the American and British Shorthair, the American Wirehair, the Birman, the Bombay, the Burmese, the Burmilla, the Chartreux, the Japanese Bobtail, the Maine Coon, the Manx and its longhaired sibling the Cymric, the Norwegian Forest Cat, the Ocicat, the Exotic Shorthair, the Ragdoll, the Scottish Fold, the Selkirk Rex, members of the Siamese family (Siamese, Balinese, Javanese, Oriental), the Siberian, the Snowshoe, the Sphynx, and the Tonkinese.

What makes these cats good with kids? The Chartreux, Maine Coon, and Norwegian Forest Cat, for instance, are sturdy, friendly, and enjoy households with lots of activity. Exotic Shorthairs and Ragdolls are placid and docile. The Ocicat and members of the Siamese family are smart, outgoing, talkative, curious, and easily trained. American and British Shorthairs are affectionate and adaptable.

Take your child's personality into consideration as well. Choose a placid breed for a quiet child and a more active or trainable breed for the child that will enjoy teaching a cat to walk on a leash or do tricks (yes, cats can learn to do tricks). Again, many domestic shorthairs and longhairs are also great with kids.

COAT OF MANY COLORS

What colors and patterns do cats come in?

That's a big question. Cats come in solid colors; tabby, tortoiseshell, calico, bicolor, and pointed patterns; and various shades of silver.

Solid colors are black, light brown, dark brown, cream, fawn, gray/blue, lilac, red/orange, and white. These colors are described as either deep or dilute. Dilute colors occur when a given color is unevenly distributed along the hair shafts. Examples are gray/blue, a dilution of black; cream, a dilution of red/orange; lilac, a dilution of dark brown; and fawn, a dilution of light brown.

Most solid-colored cats have a recessive gene that suppresses the tabby pattern. Sometimes the tabby pattern isn't completely suppressed and when the light shines just right on the cat you can see the ghosts of tabby markings.

The color white occurs when a dominant gene masks any other color the cat may have in his genetic makeup. Sometimes, kittens have a spot of what is known as breakthrough pigment on their heads. This spot, which usually fades with age, can give a clue to the cat's underlying genetic color. All-white cats can pass on their masked color genes, so they may produce kittens of other colors or patterns.

Tabby patterns are formed when agouti hairs, which have alternating bands of dark and light color, combine with nonagouti, or solid-colored, dark hairs, giving the coat an appearance of having dark stripes or spots. The four tabby patterns are the classic tabby, with swirls or circles on the sides of the body; the mackerel tabby, whose narrow dark stripes radiate downward from the middle of the back, giving rise to the nickname of tiger cat; the spotted tabby, with—natch—spots all over its sides, a distinctive coat that is worn by the Ocicat and the Egyptian Mau; and the ticked tabby, a coat made up almost entirely of agouti hairs, seen in the Abyssinian as well as nonpedigreed cats. Tabbies can come in brown, blue, red, cream, or silver. When you see a tabby cat, look for the M marking that each one bears on his forehead.

Cats with the piebald spotting gene have areas of white on their body. Cats in this category can have different forms of white spotting. Bicolor cats usually have large patches of color or patterns with white, about half and half. Van cats are mostly white with small patches of color, usually on the head and tail. Mitted cats have white paws. Cats with lockets are solid-colored with a small spot of white (the locket) on the chest. Tuxedo cats are black with a white chest, belly, and paws.

Cats that are randomly patched with different colors are tortoiseshells, patched tabbies, or calicos. Tortoiseshell cats typically have black, red, and cream hair, but a dilute tortoiseshell can have a light blue and cream coat. Some tortoiseshells have small patches of white. Torties with large amounts of white are called calicos. Tortoiseshell and calico cats are almost always female because the pattern is sex-linked.

Brown-patched tabbies, also referred to as torbies (short for tortoiseshell tabby), can resemble a pile of fallen leaves with their patches of brown and red tabby. Blue-patched tabbies have patches of blue tabby and cream tabby. A patched tabby with white is called a calico tabby, a patterned calico, or a caliby.

Points are dark areas on the face, paws, and tail, which fade to a lighter color on the body. The pointed pattern is associated with the Siamese cat, but other cat breeds and nonpedigreed cats can have points. Pointed cats are born white and develop their points as they mature. Points can be solid or patterned and come in many different colors, including sealpoint (dark brown points with a light brown to ivory body), blue point (gray points with a light gray or beige body), lynx point (tabby points with a brown, blue, red, cream, or silver body), and tortie point (tortoiseshell points with a cream-colored body). Silver cats have a gene mutation that removes the yellowish-tan pigment from the cat's hair. They come in several varieties: smoke, shaded, chinchilla, and silver tabby. Smokes are solid black or gray cats whose hair roots are distinctly white. Shaded cats are ticked tabbies with lighter, wider agouti bands. The result is a hair shaft that's colored at the tip and lighter below the tip. A chinchilla coat is one in which all the hairs are lightly colored at the tip, becoming lighter below the tip. Chinchillas appear white at first glance, but a closer look shows their subtle coloring. A silver tabby has ticked hairs that are tipped with black, blue, cream, or red, shading to a lighter, almost white color below the tip. The solid hairs have normal coloration, creating a striking contrast.

Cats come in an infinite variety of colors and patterns.

There's a lot more to know about cat colors and the genetics of color in cats. For more information, see www.fanciers.com/other-faqs/color-genetics.html.

SNEEZE-FREE KITTY?

I have allergies, but I'd still like to have a cat. Are there any breeds that are hypoallergenic? If not, are there ways I can live comfortably with a cat?

Although hairless and wire-coated breeds are often touted as being suitable for people with allergies, no specific breed of cat is guaranteed not to cause reactions in people who are sensitive to cat allergens. Indeed, it's not the cat's fur that causes allergies but the proteins found in the hair, saliva, and dander (dead skin flakes). The hair and dander mix with house dust—itself containing multiple allergens such as dust mites and molds—and wafts through the air, landing on the lining of the eyes or nose. It can also be inhaled directly into the lungs. All cats produce dander, even hairless ones, and of course all cats have saliva, so there's no escaping the presence of allergenic proteins.

If you are determined to have a cat, you may find that bathing the cat weekly helps keep dander levels low. Be sure to use a shampoo that won't dry out your cat's skin. Dryness causes itching and scratching, which in turn produces more dander. There are also sprays on the market that claim to reduce or remove pet dander. The solution is sprayed onto a cloth or towel and wiped onto the cat to remove dander. These sprays may or may not work for you, but it can't hurt to try them. They can take several weeks to be effective, so give them time to work. You may need to apply the spray daily or weekly, depending on your individual situation. Look for these topical sprays or liquids at pet supply stores or veterinary clinics.

Most allergists recommend keeping at least one room in the house pet-free, usually the bedroom. Avoiding direct contact with the cat's fur can also be helpful since allergens can be absorbed through skin as well as inhaled. If these steps aren't possible, wash bedding—yours and the cat's—and soft cat toys frequently in hot water, at least 130 degrees Fahrenheit. Cover mattresses, pillows, and cushions in allergen-resistant plastic, and cover furniture with a throw that can be washed often or with washable slipcovers. Wash your hands after touching your cat.

While you might think that frequent vacuuming is a good idea, most vacuum cleaners aren't able to get deep down into carpets where allergens settle and can even stir up allergen particles. To get around this problem, try using a HEPA vacuum filter or double bags, and change bags and filters frequently. Better yet, let someone else vacuum while you're out of the house. The best solution might be to get rid of carpeting altogether and install a hardwood, tile or linoleum floor. Cloth curtains and blinds also catch and hold allergens, so consider replacing them with other window coverings such as wood or plastic blinds.

Keep the air in your home fresh. Reactions often worsen in winter when windows and doors are kept shut. It may help to install ventilated filters on the furnace or air ducts. Using a HEPA room air filter can also help remove airborne allergens.

A lot depends on how severe your allergies are and how much you're willing to put up with for the pleasure of having a cat. Be aware that many breeders will not sell cats to allergic individuals, for fear that the cat will be returned, given away, or abandoned at a shelter. For more information on allergies to cats, visit the following Web site: www.allergies.about.com/library/weekly/aa013100a.htm.

MEET THE FAMILY

If I'm buying a pedigreed kitten, is it a good idea to meet the kitten's parents? What if only the mother is available?

Meeting the parents helps you gauge what a kitten's temperament will be like. If the parents are laid-back and charming, your kitten is likely to follow in their pawprints. If the parents are shy or aggressive, their kittens will probably have similar faults in temperament. Observe the breeder's other adult cats. They, too, can give you a clue as to what your kitten will be like when he matures.

Often, only the mother cat is on the breeders' premises. If the father is from out of town, or is confined elsewhere in the cattery (stud males can be temperamental), ask to see pictures or videos of him. The breeder shouldn't have any problem producing these visuals for you. Ask what his temperament is like as well.

NOT FOR SALE

The breeder won't let me have the kitten I like best. Why not?

There are a couple of reasons the breeder might have vetoed your choice. One is that she plans to show that kitten. Unless you're interested in ponying up the costs for entry fees and travel to show sites, she won't want to sell you a show-quality kitten. Many breeders don't even let people see the kittens that aren't available, for exactly this reason: people fall in love with the prettiest of the kitties and then are disappointed when they can't have her.

Another reason might be that the breeder believes that a different kitten is more suited to your home life or personality. The breeder has been watching the kittens for a couple of months, and she has a pretty good idea of which ones will do best in which homes. A rambunctious kitten will do better in a family with kids and dogs than with a retired couple, while a quiet, reserved kitten that might be overwhelmed by all those kids and dogs is perfect for a pair of senior citizens who want a sweet, laid-back cat.

Politely ask the breeder to explain her reasons for refusing you the kitten, and be willing to respect her judgment. If you still disagree with her assessment, consider finding a different breeder.

SHY AWAY

I've fallen in love with a sweet cat at the shelter, but he's very shy. My friend says I shouldn't get him. Do you think she's right?

Shy cats can be very appealing. They seem vulnerable, and that appeals to our nurturing instincts. On the other hand, shy cats usually have had little contact with people or they've been badly treated by people in the past. It takes a lot of time and patience to build a relationship with a shy cat. Questions to ask yourself before deciding to adopt this cat include the following:

- Are you willing to place the cat's needs above your own?
- Are you willing to accept a cat that might not behave the way you expect a cat to?
- Can you accept it if the cat doesn't want to sit on your lap or be close to you?
- Do you have the patience and persistence to help bring a shy cat out of his shell?
- Is your home relatively calm or are you overrun with loud, active children and dogs?
- Is someone home during the day who will enjoy spending time with the cat?
- Do you have another, more confident cat who can show the shy cat the ropes?

Shy cats can take months or even years to learn to live comfortably with people. They often hide, especially when strangers come to the home, and they dislike loud noises. It took a good ten years before my domestic longhair, Shelby, quit running whenever she heard the doorbell ring. And even more so than other cats, shy cats like a predictable routine.

Nonetheless, if you are willing to take on the effort required to make friends with a shy cat, you can be rewarded by a purrfectly wonderful relationship. That's what Maryjean Ballner discovered when she met four-year-old Boots, who had been rescued from a condemned home where he had been living with twenty-six other cats. Boots was so fearful of people that shelter staff recommended he be euthanized because of the improbability of finding him the right home. But Ballner wanted to give him a chance.

"He stayed upstairs in my office for the first three months," Ballner says. "He cringed whenever I came near him, but every day I wrapped him in a towel and massaged him. He finally got to the point where he would come out of the office and go downstairs, but as soon as we moved, he would run back upstairs and hide."

Ballner renamed Boots, calling him Bodacious, and with time and the guidance of Ballner's other cat, Champ, he became more confident. Now, three years later, when Ballner lies on her loveseat, Bo sits on her chest and purrs.

CONTRACT BASICS

The breeder wants me to sign a contract. What should I expect?

Contracts vary from breeder to breeder, but in general they require the buyer to keep the cat indoors, to spay or neuter a pet-quality kitten (if the breeder hasn't already had this surgery performed), and to return the cat to the breeder if there's ever a reason you can't keep him. Often a contract prohibits declawing. It may also state that the breeder will withhold registration papers until she receives proof that a pet-quality kitten has been spayed or neutered. The contract should state whether you have breeding rights or that the kitten is being sold on a not-for-breeding basis. Some contracts describe the kitten and note the gender, date of birth, and parents' names.

If you are purchasing a show-quality kitten, the contract may call for you to show or breed the kitten, or may name the breeder as the kitten's co-owner, giving her say over the kitten's future. This may be acceptable to you if you're interested in showing and breeding, but be aware that co-ownerships can go sour. Be sure the breeder is someone that you can work with over the long term.

For your protection, a contract should also include a written health guarantee, as well as a stipulation that you take the cat to your veterinarian for an exam within forty-eight hours of purchase to ensure that the kitten is in good health at the time of purchase. If the kitten does have a problem, the contract should spell out whether the breeder will pay for the kitten's care or exchange him for another one.

These contracts are valid and will stand up in a court of law. Don't sign one if you're not willing to abide by the terms.

Not in the contract but a heartfelt desire of many breeders is that you keep in touch during your cat's life. "I love to see pictures of my kittens," Vella says. "I get pictures at Christmas every year of the cats we've sold as pets, and it's one of the most delightful things in the world."

PAPER CHASE

What are "papers" and what should I expect to receive from the breeder?

If you are buying a pedigreed kitten, the breeder should provide you with a three-generation pedigree (the kitten's family tree) and registration papers proving that the kitten is of a particular breed and qualifies to be registered with, say, CFA or TICA. The breeder registers each litter with a particular registry and in return receives an individual registration form for each kitten. She should give you this form when you take your kitten home (or when you provide proof that the kitten has been spayed or neutered).

Fill out the registration form with your kitten's name, and mail it to the registry with the appropriate fee. The registry will send you the kitten's registration papers, which you can frame or put in his kitten baby book.

What good are registration papers and a pedigree? They don't guarantee that your kitten will be perfect, but they usually indicate that you're dealing with a reputable breeder and that you're getting what you're paying for. Breeders who can't provide registration papers may have bred cats that were sold without breeding rights (pet-quality cats). Even if you are purchasing a pet-quality kitten, you should still expect to receive this documentation.

Other paperwork you may receive from the breeder is the kitten's health records, noting which vaccinations have been given, and when, as well as the deworming schedule and any other pertinent health information. Take this information to your veterinarian on the kitten's first visit. The breeder may also give you a fact sheet detailing what the kitten eats, how often he eats, what kind of litter he's used to using, the history of his breed, tips on training, and other helpful information.

CONTRACTS AND SHELTER ADOPTIONS

Will I have to sign a contract if I adopt a cat from an animal shelter or a breed-rescue group? What is it likely to require, and do I have to abide by it?

The adoption contract in Appendix II used by the Hillside SPCA in Pottsville, Pennsylvania, is typical of what you might encounter in such a document. It calls for the adopter to keep cats indoors at all times unless a screened-in porch or similar enclosure is available. The adopter agrees to have the cat spayed or neutered by a specified date, to provide proper veterinary care, and to permit the SPCA to visit the home to check on the cat's health and verify that he has been neutered. The shelter can reclaim the cat if he's not receiving adequate care or if he hasn't been neutered by the agreed-upon date.

The contract also states that all family members have agreed to the adoption and will abide by the terms of the agreement. Adopters must be at least eighteen years old and never subject to legal action for cruelty to or neglect of animals.

Tenants must have written permission from their landlord consenting to the cat's adoption. The cat must be returned to the shelter if the adopter is ever unable to care for him. Adopters are not permitted to sell the cat or give him to someone else without written consent from the shelter. A contract is a contract, and if you sign one, you are expected to abide by its terms.

REHOMING A CAT

When you get a cat, it should be with the understanding that you are taking on the responsibility for the cat for the rest of his life. That's not a short-term commitment, but in exchange you get years of love and devotion. Sometimes, however, life doesn't always work out the way we'd like it to. A family crisis such as divorce, illness, or death may mean that you need to place the cat in a new home. What if you get a cat and weeks, months, or even years later, a situation occurs that no longer makes it possible for you to keep your cat?

If you have a pedigreed cat, your first step should be to contact the breeder. If she truly has an interest in her cats' welfare, she will take him back or help you find a new home for him, even if he's no longer a kitten. "We always hope that the homes where we place our kittens are their 'forever homes,' but we understand that sometimes things happen to change that, and we'd like to help in their rehoming," says Maine Coon breeder Donna Day. This is one of the many good reasons for keeping in touch with your cat's breeder.

What if you have a domestic shorthair or longhair who didn't come from a breeder? Start by trying to place your cat with a responsible family member or friend. This can allow you to stay involved with your cat's welfare. If that's not possible, try posting a notice at your veterinarian's office or your pet supply store. A flyer with your cat's picture, plus information about his age, gender, personality, and good qualities (litter-box trained, spayed/neutered, good with kids and dogs, likes to sit in laps) can help land him a fine new home.

Thoroughly screen potential owners to ensure that your cat goes to a loving home. If possible, visit the adopter's home and get references from his or her veterinarian. Some unscrupulous people pose as adopters and then sell pets to laboratories for research. For this reason, it's best to avoid the phrase "free to a good home." Someone who is willing to pay a small adoption fee is more likely to be committed to giving your cat a good home.

Another option is to place a profile of your cat on an adoption Web site such as petfinder.com. With luck, your orange-eyed gray cat will be just what someone else is looking for.

When you've found a new home, help ease your cat's transition by providing his new owners with a written description of his habits, likes and dislikes, favorite food, toys, and litter, and so on. Include your veterinarian's phone number and your cat's veterinary records. Finally, before you leave him, make sure he's wearing a tag with the new owners' name and phone number, in case he escapes from their home. If possible, check back occasionally to see how he's doing. This will help ease your mind about his welfare.

KITTY DICTIONARY: TERMS TO KNOW

If you're buying a pedigreed cat, you'll probably hear the breeder use some terms that you might not be familiar with. Here's a guide to some of the most common terms and what they mean.

Blue slip: an application to register a cat from a registered litter (what you will receive from the breeder)

Breed standard: the ideal characteristics of a particular breed, as agreed upon by a group of breeders

Breeding quality: a cat that is valuable for a breeding program but doesn't have the qualities needed to succeed in the show ring

Cattery: a multiple-cat household maintained for the purpose of perpetuating and protecting the heritage and desirable traits of the various breeds of pedigreed cats

Dam: the mother of a litter

Domestic longhair: a longhaired cat of unknown parentage

Domestic shorthair: a shorthaired cat of unknown parentage

Heat: a female's estrus period, during which time she is fertile and receptive to a male's advances

Household pet: a class at a cat show open to all cats, pedigreed or not, that are not eligible to compete in any other class

National award: given to cats that earn enough points during a show year to be ranked among the highest scoring cats in the entire association for that year

Neuter: to castrate a male cat

Not for breeding: a cat that has been designated by the breeder as not to be used for breeding and whose offspring, if produced, cannot be registered

Odd-eyed: a cat with one blue eye and one green, gold, or copper eye

Papers: a cat's pedigree and registration slip

Pedigree: a cat's family tree, showing three to five generations

Pet quality: a cat that does not meet the breed standard closely enough to be valuable to a breeding program

Queen: a whole female cat (see "Whole" below)

Regional award: given to cats that earn enough points during a show year to be ranked among the highest scoring cats in a particular region for that year

Registered cat: one whose ancestry is documented and recorded with a cat registry, such as ACFA, CFA, or TICA

Registered name: a registered cat's official name, which can include titles and cattery names

Show quality: a cat that meets the breed standard closely enough to be competitive at cat shows

Sire: the father of a litter

Spay: to surgically remove a female cat's reproductive organs, sometimes referred to as an ovariohysterectomy

Stud: a male cat used for breeding

Tom: a whole male cat

Whole: not spayed or neutered

CHAPTER 4

Shopping for Your New Cat

THE KITTEN OR CAT of your dreams is finally at hand. After months of researching breeds, interviewing breeders, or scouring the animal shelter, you have found the perfect cat and he's ready to go home with you.

But are you ready to bring him home? Just as new mothers prepare a layette for their babies, so must new cat owners lay in a supply of items necessary for the care and safety of their cat. Before you bring your new kitten or cat home, be sure you have the following supplies on hand:

- Collar and tag. Order a tag engraved with your name and telephone number several weeks before you bring your kitten home. Attach it to a breakaway collar—one that will slip safely off the kitten's head should he become hung up on something. Put the collar and tag on the kitten before you leave the breeder's home or the shelter. You should be able to fit two fingers between the collar and the cat's neck.

- Carrier. Columbus, Drake, Magellan . . . none of them can hold a candle to the kitten, the boldest explorer of them all. But a car in motion is not the place for a young cat (or a cat of any age) to be roaming free. You will need a crate or soft-sided carrier to contain the kitten for the ride to his new home, as well as for visits to the veterinarian, the groomer, and Grandma's house.

- Litter box. Pet supply stores carry a variety of litter box styles. The one you choose depends on where you plan to place the box, as well as personal preference. An open litter box is easy to evaluate for cleanliness and easy to scoop, but a burrowing kitten can quickly make a mess, scattering litter everywhere. Covered litter boxes help contain odor and mess and provide the cat with privacy. More elaborate litter boxes come with self-scooping systems and a litter tray that lifts out for disposal of solid waste.

- Litter. Ask the breeder what type of litter the kitten has been using. Start with that litter so your kitten will be comfortable with its scent and texture. Cats can be finicky about those things. Once your kitten is using the litter box regularly, you can gradually switch to a different litter if you prefer another brand or type. Most cats are turned off by heavily scented litters or show a slight allergic reaction to the scent, so you're better off choosing one that's unscented or only lightly scented.

- Food. To fuel his growth, a kitten needs food containing high-quality protein. Ask the breeder what she's been feeding and start with that brand. If you want to switch, your veterinarian can give you some recommendations. In general, however, look for a food that is specially formulated for kittens. Be sure to choose one that's labeled as complete and balanced. Ideally, the label will state that the manufacturer has used feeding trials to substantiate the food's nutritional value. In other words, the company fed the diet to a number of cats over a given period to make sure they thrived and grew on it. In chapter eight, you'll find detailed information on evaluating cat foods as well as a discussion of the pros and cons of homemade and raw diets.

- Treats. Treats are a great way to make friends with your kitten and reward her for good behavior. And it's just fun to give a cat something special once in a while. Look for more on treats in chapter eight.
- Dishes. You'll need one dish for food and one for water. It's nice to have a second set to use when the first set is in the dishwasher. Stainless steel bowls are usually recommended for ease of cleaning.
- Grooming items. The basics you'll need are a flea comb, a wire slicker brush or rubber curry brush, a nail trimmer, and a toothbrush and toothpaste. You'll find more about grooming in chapter nine.
- Toys. The energy expended by a kitten could light up Las Vegas. To channel that energy, provide toys that will exercise not only the kitten's body but also her brain. Look for toys that are sturdy, without small parts that can be bitten off or shredded by claws.
- Bed. Your kitten will enjoy having a soft place to curl up and catnap after playtime. From tepees to tunnels, cushions to custom couches, you can find an infinite variety of beds that will suit not only your cat but also your décor. Choose a bed that's well-constructed and machine washable.

You can find all of these items at your local pet supply store. You can also purchase kitty paraphernalia online and have it delivered if that's more convenient. Simply do a Web search for "cat supplies" to find any number of sources that will meet your cat-care needs. The following questions and answers will help you purchase appropriate items.

CRATE EXPECTATIONS

What should I look for in a cat carrier? Is it better to get one that's hard-sided or soft-sided?

Personal preference and your cat's future lifestyle are factors to consider. You'll want a sturdy carrier that will hold your kitten comfortably and keep him safe in case of an accident.

Crates made of plastic are tough, long lasting, and easy to clean. They're suitable for air travel if your cat will be living a globe-trotter lifestyle, and they can be secured in a car by running the seatbelt through the handle on the top of the crate.

Soft-sided carriers are comfortable and easy to transport. The zippered top and end closures make it easy to place the cat in and remove him from the carrier. They're also durable and easy to clean. On airlines, soft-sided models are acceptable carriers for cats traveling in the cabin, but they can't be used if the cat is traveling in cargo (a situation best avoided, anyway).

COLLAR CONNECTION

How do I measure my kitten's neck to make sure I get the right size collar?

Use a cloth tape measure to determine the circumference of your cat's neck. Add one inch to that measurement to ensure that the collar isn't too tight. You should be able to slip two fingers comfortably between the collar and the kitten's neck. As your kitten grows, check the collar frequently to make sure it isn't too tight and adjust it accordingly.

SAFETY FEATURES

What is a breakaway collar and why does my cat need one?

Cats are adventurous and they love to climb. It's not unusual for them to try to squeeze through a narrow opening or to climb up on something where the collar could get hung up and choke them. Some collars have what is called a breakaway clip, which releases if the cat gets caught on something. Others are made of stretchy material that allows them to pull off if the cat becomes entangled. You can find breakaway or safety collars at just about any pet supply store.

A GOOD ID

I'm not planning on letting my cat go outdoors. Does she really need a collar and tags, let alone one of those ID microchips I've heard about?

"The best laid schemes o' mice and men gang aft a-gley." Scottish poet Robert Burns knew what he was talking about. No matter how careful you are, there is always the possibility that your cat can get outside. Workmen can leave the door open, or the door can close but not latch, allowing kitty to push it open. There are any number of ways that your cat can get outside without your knowing it. We still have never figured out how our cat Pandora escaped one evening, nor how she found her way back inside three days later. And we would leave our cat Peter safely secured inside our apartment, only to find him lounging outdoors when we returned home from work. He was, we discovered, flipping open the louvered windows in the bathroom and slipping out.

So yes, your cat does need a collar and tags. They're the first line of identification when a cat is found. Put your name and phone number on the tag. If there's room, include your work or cell phone number as well, or your veterinarian's phone number. But collars and tags can come off. Some cats are Houdinis, able to get out of any collar. Others may have their collars removed for them, by someone who wants to keep the cat for herself. A microchip is a high-tech method of ensuring that your cat can still be identified, even without his collar and tags. A microchip provides permanent identification that can't be removed. It's tiny, about the size of a grain of rice, and programmed with a unique, unalterable code number, as well as the electronic circuitry required to send out the code number. A microchip will last your cat's lifetime, without ever needing any kind of recharging.

Your veterinarian can implant a microchip when your cat is twelve weeks or older. It's injected beneath the skin in the scruff of the neck, between the shoulder blades. The injection is no more painful than a vaccination, and no sedation or anesthesia is required. The microchip sends a signal when it's activated by a scanning device. Scanners are widely available at many animal shelters and veterinary clinics. If your cat is found and taken to a shelter or veterinary clinic, he can be scanned, identified, and returned to you quickly. According to statistics from the Honolulu Humane Society, nearly 100 percent of the cats found there that have microchip IDs are reunited with their people. A San Francisco newspaper recently reported a story about a cat that was returned to his owner ten years after he wandered off, thanks to his microchip.

You can list your microchipped cat with a national registry, which usually provides twenty-four-hour notification, a tag notifying finders that the cat is microchipped, and instructions on how to contact the registry. Be sure to notify the registry any time your address changes. If you choose not to register your cat, the vet or shelter that scans him can still get in touch with you by notifying the veterinarian who implanted the chip, assuming your address hasn't changed.

DISHING ABOUT DISHES

There are so many types of food and water dishes for cats. What should I buy?

Food and water dishes come in a variety of materials. Each has advantages and disadvantages. Read on to find out what will work best for you.

Metal bowls are utilitarian. They last indefinitely and are easy to clean. One drawback is that they can't be used to heat food in the microwave. Another is that they are lightweight, making it easy for rowdy kittens to bat them around on the floor, spilling water and food. You can, however, find metal dishes with rubber nonskid rims on the bottom. Others have weighted bottoms so they don't tip easily.

Ceramic dishes are decorative and can be personalized. Generally, they're dishwasher and microwave safe. They are heavy, making them more stable, but they're also breakable. Some ceramic dishes made outside the United States contain high amounts of lead and should not be used by people or animals.

Plastic dishes are colorful and inexpensive. Like ceramic dishes, they're dishwasher safe, and like metal dishes, they're lightweight. Some cats have allergic reactions to plastic, resulting in a condition called feline chin acne, so many cat experts advise against using plastic dishes. The nicks in a plastic bowl can also trap food debris, making cleaning difficult.

AN OLD YARN

My mother says not to waste money on toys because a ball of yarn will keep my cat entertained just fine. Is she right?

In this case, mother doesn't always know best. Cats do love playing with and chasing yarn, but it's dangerous if swallowed (which isn't unusual). Many cats, especially those in the Siamese family, enjoy sucking on wool and yarn. When they swallow it, the yarn can become entangled in their intestines or cause an obstruction, which can be fatal if the problem isn't discovered and surgically remedied in time. The same is true of string, thread, rubber bands, and similar items. Twist ties, a favorite cat play item, can perforate the intestines if swallowed.

For some fun and safe homemade cat toys, tie a long piece of string to a wadded-up piece of paper and pull it for your cat to chase. Put it away when you're not there to supervise. Aluminum-foil balls are another feline favorite. Simply wad up some aluminum foil into a ball and let your cat bat it around on the floor. Make the ball large enough that the cat can't swallow it, and pack the foil tightly so there aren't any loose bits that could be chewed up and swallowed.

KEEPING KITTY ENTERTAINED

What are the best toys for my cat?

Cats are curious and athletic. They love any toy that will challenge their mind, make use of their innate hunting skills, or involve lots of hockey-style sliding and body slamming. Sharpen those feline hunting skills and develop acrobatic ability with a fishing-pole-type toy. The amazing flips and spins this type of toy elicits will keep you and your kitten entertained for hours. Even older cats love these toys and will pace and cry in front of the closet where they're stored, begging you to bring them out. This is a great way for you and your cat to interact, without much effort on your part. You can swing it around while you're lying in your recliner watching television, although some cats prefer that you drag it behind you so they can chase it.

A stuffed mouse, especially one that makes a squeaking sound when pounced on or is scented with catnip, will intrigue any cat. A windup mouse that moves on its own is even better. Some toy mice are made of fur (fake or otherwise), which is attractive to cats. Others are connected to a stand by a spring and can be batted around by the cat.

Cats love anything in motion, so balls of all kinds are big favorites. Roll a ping-pong ball, super ball, glitter ball, or a plastic ball with a noisemaker inside it and watch your cat go after it. This is especially fun on a hard floor. Make sure the ball is large enough that your cat can't swallow it.

A ping-pong ball inside a circular plastic track helps develop motor skills as your kitten or cat attempts to bat it around the track.

Choose toys that are made specifically for cats. They're less likely to have small parts that could come off and be swallowed. Eyes and tails on toy mice, for instance, should be sewn on tightly. Never leave your kitten or cat alone with any toy that has a string or cord attached, such as a fishing-pole toy. Swallowing string can be fatal.

STRING THEORY

I know it's dangerous for kittens to swallow string or yarn. What should I do if I see some hanging out of my cat's mouth?

Don't try to pull it out. That can cause more damage. Take the cat to the veterinarian right away. Surgery may be necessary to remove the string safely.

THE SKINNY ON SCRATCHING

My neighbor says I should get a tall scratching post wrapped in rope instead of carpet. What's so great about rope, and why does a little kitten need a three-foot post?

The ideal scratching post is indeed about three feet high—or higher! This height allows a grown cat to stretch out to his full length when scratching. Scratching is a way for cats to mark their territory, and the higher they can scratch, the bigger and more important they feel. Three feet or more is also a great height for a kitten to scamper up. Some posts have an area at the top where the cat can sit, surveying her domain. Until they got very old, my cats liked to sit on top of their post and supervise while I cooked dinner. They also used it as a stepping stone to other areas, such as windowsills or the top of the bookcase.

Why rope? Its texture is attractive to cats and it's different from other household surfaces, such as carpets or upholstered furniture. If you get your cat a post wrapped in carpet, he won't see any difference between that and the carpet on the floor and will scratch on both equally.

The benefit of a scratching post—besides the protection of your carpet and upholstery—is that it helps your cat sharpen his claws and shed old claw coverings. I'm always finding little claw remains at the base of my cat's post. You still need to trim your cat's claws to keep them at a manageable—and safe—length, but a scratching post will help keep them in shape as well. Scratching is also a territorial imperative: the scent glands on a cat's paw pads let other animals know that this is his space.

To entice your cat to use the post, run your fingers up and down it. The sound and motion will attract him and he'll pounce on it. Be sure your hand is out of the way! Once he's clawing on it, give him lots of praise. Reward him with praise or petting every time you see him using it. Any time you see him scratching on something he shouldn't, don't yell; simply pick him up, take him to his post and encourage him to use it. Praise him when he does.

You can purchase—or make—a simple scratching post of the appropriate size at most pet supply stores or at a cat show (see the boxed story at the end of this chapter). Some rope/sisal scratching boards are designed to hang on a doorknob or lie flat on the floor (some cats like to stretch out horizontally when they scratch). Other good scratching surfaces include cardboard boxes, lumber, or logs. Be sure that whatever you use is firmly anchored so that it doesn't wobble or roll when the cat uses it.

If you want to go all out, attend a cat show to check out the deluxe cat trees that are available. Seren, a Siamese who owns cat writer Amy Shojai, has a three-tiered cat tree with three vertical cedar posts. "It's a kitty scratching favorite, sleeping favorite, and throne all rolled into one," Shojai says.

Provide your cat with a tall scratching post that allows him to stretch to his full length.

THE CAT'S MEOW

Why do cats go crazy for catnip? My kitten doesn't seem that interested in it, but my friend's cat loves it.

Catnip is an herb that belongs to the mint family. Its scientific name is *Nepeta cataria*. The crazy-making compound in catnip is called nepetalactone, which mimics the scent of a cat's sex pheromones. The behavior of cats under the influence of catnip—rolling, yowling, and rubbing, for instance—is definitely similar to the behaviors they show when they're sexually aroused. It's sort of a kitty aphrodisiac, although it can't elicit actual sexual behavior since that is hormonally controlled.

A catnip high (which is harmless) usually lasts five to fifteen minutes, after which the effects start to wear off. Fresh catnip gets the best reaction. Your kitten may be too young, however, to respond to catnip. Kittens younger than three months of age—and very old cats—usually don't show a response to catnip. Perhaps it's because they haven't yet reached adolescence—in the case of kittens—or because they've gone through the kitty equivalent of menopause. Your kitten may also be one of the 10 to 30 percent of cats that don't show any interest in catnip, due to a genetic anomaly. Wait until your kitten is a little older, and try offering her catnip again. She may love it. If she does, catnip is easy to grow. You can keep a plant on hand so she always has a stash.

CAT NAPS

Does my cat need a bed? I was going to let her sleep on the bed with me.

Letting your cat sleep on the bed with you is fine as long as you don't have allergies and don't mind a soft little paw gently—or not so gently—tapping you awake in the morning. During the day, your cat will spend time napping on various pieces of furniture, from the sofa to the armchair to the top of the refrigerator (where it's nice and warm). Nonetheless, your cat will also enjoy a little bed in a corner or out-of-the-way spot. Cats enjoy hiding out in small, enclosed areas, so he'll think that a bed underneath a table or an enclosed tepee or igloo-style bed is the cat's pajamas. It's not a necessity, of course, but it will give him added comfort and security in his new home.

GETTING THE GOODS AT CAT SHOWS

If you love to shop and you have a new cat, a cat show is a terrific place to purchase all the feline accoutrements your cat could ever need or want. From carriers to castles, feather wands to fur mice, litter to literally anything cat-related you can think of, you'll find it at a cat show. Besides the variety and quality of the items sold at cat shows, you can usually count on show discounts to help relieve the dent in your wallet. And you can count on lots of cat-loving folks being there to offer opinions and experiences with the kitty paraphernalia, says veteran cat lover Amy Shojai of Sherman, Texas.

When Darlene Arden of Framingham, Massachusetts, acquired her Chartreux, Aimee, her friend Shojai stepped in as equipment advisor and took her shopping at a cat show. "We left a lot of giddy vendors in our wake," Arden reports. Aimee went to her new home with an assortment of feather toys, glitter balls, and more, plus a Sturdibag for the trip on the airplane.

Arden's latest purchase for Aimee was a terrific cat tree that she found at a show. "I bought the biggest one I could afford and that I could haul out of the car and into the house," she says. "Aimee adores it. It's big, sturdy, and has three beds on different levels. The top and middle ones are open, and the bottom one is a barrel bed with a window cutout. The carpet on it is beautiful, and the posts are sisal. It's very sturdy and you wouldn't find it in most pet supply stores." Aimee also loves pipe-cleaner toys, catnip toys, and her slanted scratching post (from the same vendor that made her new cat tree), all of which Arden purchased at cat shows.

CHAPTER **5**

Preparing Your Home for Your New Cat

THE FIRST STEP in living successfully with a cat—especially a kitten—is to make sure your home is safe from him and that he's safe from your home. Cats and kittens love to explore, and you'd be amazed at some of the places and things their curiosity can lead them to. Besides ensuring your cat's safety, you'll want to make decisions about where he'll eat, sleep, and use the litter box.

Kittens may look sweet and innocent, but the amount of trouble they can get into in just a short period of time is mind-boggling. One minute they're rolling around on the floor wrestling with a toy mouse, the next thing you know they're climbing the curtains—the really expensive ones that you just had custom made. Kittens will climb up or jump onto anything tall given the least bit of opportunity, and they'll crawl under or inside anything that looks dark and cozy, from reclining chairs to clothes dryers. They'll swallow small objects, jump out windows—unaware of the twenty-story drop—and fall into toilets. Before you bring your kitten home, take a walk through the house and make note of everything that could pose a hazard to your kitten or that your kitten could destroy during her explorations. Make sure doors latch securely and screens are hole-free.

This is also the time to decide where you'll feed him and where to put the litter box. Usually, the kitchen is the most convenient place for kitty meals. That's where the food is, after all, assuming you store it in the pantry. It's also convenient for filling up water dishes, throwing away empty cans or bags, and putting dirty dishes in the dishwasher. Just as you wouldn't want to eat off smelly, food-encrusted plates, neither does your cat, with his highly sensitive nose. Wherever you decide to feed your cat, it should be a quiet, pleasant area, with no noises or disturbances that might interrupt his meal or frighten him while he's eating.

Next, decide where to put his litter box. The main thing to remember is that it should be well away from his food and water dishes. Cats are fastidious, and they don't like to eat and eliminate in the same place. A bathroom can be a good choice, because it's easy to just dump what you scoop into the toilet and flush it away (assuming you're using flushable litter).

What about all those cat naps? Does your kitten or cat need a specific place to sleep? Unless someone in the family has allergies, there's nothing wrong with letting the cat sleep in the bedroom—on or off the bed. Especially for a kitten who's away from her mother and littermates for the first time, sleeping in the bedroom can be comforting. If you don't want her on the bed, however, you will need to gently remove her from it every time she jumps up there until she learns it's off limits. That can make for a lot of long nights, and many people give up before the cat does. You'll have to be consistent and persistent if you want to win this one. Besides, a cat's soothing purr can help you fall asleep, and his furry coat will help keep you warm on chilly nights. If those advantages aren't appealing (and if they're not, you may want to rethink getting a cat), you may prefer that the cat sleep outside the bedroom at night. You can provide a bed, which your cat may or may not use, in a cozy area or in his safe room. Be sure he has access to water and the litter box during the night.

Kitten-proofing is also an issue when the holidays roll around. Naturally, you'll want to include your cat in your holiday celebrations. She's a special member of the family, after all. But most holidays hold at least a few hazards that you should be aware of so you can make them festive and problem-free.

In all its myriad elements, kitten-proofing prevents injuries to your kitten and to your possessions. Read on to find out the specifics that will help you turn your home into a cat-safe castle.

THE ART OF CAT PROOFING

What steps do I need to take to protect my belongings from my kitten or cat?

Start by putting away special items that are fragile or irreplaceable because of sentimental value. Take Great-Grandma's 125-year-old vases off the mantel until you can evaluate your kitten or cat's level of clumsiness. We think of cats as being graceful and good jumpers. In general, that's true, but there are exceptions. Our cat Pandora was clumsy as a kitten, and she never outgrew it. She knocked a figurine off the mantel, breaking it, chipped a couple of teacups when she knocked them off the bookshelf, and scratched up the drywall beneath the bedroom windows. A clumsy jump or switching tail can break something precious in an instant. An alternative is to use earthquake putty or picture adhesive to help keep breakable items stable. Look for it at hardware or housewares stores.

Cats and kittens love to nibble on plants (and then throw up the remains). Remove any that are toxic or that you just don't want eaten. See the lists of toxic and nontoxic plants later in this chapter. Grow some catnip or grass to satisfy your cat's craving for greens.

Put away or secure anything you don't want broken.

Kittens are little vandals who think knocking over trash cans is fun. Cover trash cans or put them behind closed doors.

Put small objects that can be swallowed out of reach as well. Keep them behind closed doors so kitty can't get to them.

KEEPING YOUR CAT SAFE

What are some other ways I can kitten-proof my house?

Walk through each room, examining it for potential hazards. Obvious hazards in every room are electrical cords. Kittens teethe, just like puppies, and they chew to relieve the pain. To protect them from a shocking experience, unplug any cords that you can, bundle cords with tough plastic cable ties and put them out of reach if possible (so they don't dangle invitingly), or spray cords with Bitter Apple or some other nasty-tasting substance. You can also encase cords in hard plastic or rubber covers available at hardware stores. Dog owners are advised to get down on their hands and knees to look for things on the floor that might attract a puppy's attention. That's good advice for kittens and cats, too, but don't forget to look up high for dangerous or unstable objects as well.

- In the kitchen. Put food away, especially meat. Cats aren't above stealing the steak that's thawing on the counter. They'll also eat—or at least lick—butter that's left out to soften. Cooked bones can splinter and cause choking or intestinal obstructions. Fatty foods can lead to a case of pancreatitis, an inflammation of the pancreas that can be serious. Raiding the trash can give your cat a case of "garbageitis," also known as gastrointestinal upset.

  Keep a close eye on your kitten when he's "helping" you cook dinner. It takes only a second for him to jump up on a hot stove and burn his paws.

  Paper grocery bags are wonderful cat toys—cats love the rustling sound they make when they're pounced on or crawled inside—but keep plastic bags out of reach. Kittens can suffocate if they get stuck inside them. Our cat Peter—the handsome gray fellow on the cover—used to enjoy playing with plastic bags until he got one stuck on his head once and couldn't get it off. He tore through the house frantically with the bag flapping behind him. After we were able to stop laughing and rescue him, he never went near one again.

- In the bathroom. Keep toilet lids down. Some cats and kittens like to drink out of the toilet. Others are fascinated by the swirling motion of the water as it's flushed away. You don't want your kitten falling into the toilet or drinking out of one that contains toxic toilet bowl cleaner.

  Don't forget to put away cosmetics, medications, and shampoos. For instance, acetaminophen, ibuprofen, and aspirin are highly toxic to cats. Pick up pills that have fallen on the floor and dispose of them in a trash can with a secure lid.

• In the laundry room. Close the dryer door as soon as you remove the clothes. A warm dryer is an inviting spot for a cat to nap. It can turn into a deadly spot, though, if you turn it on without checking to see if the cat is inside. Keep the lid down on the washer, too. We have a photo of our first two kittens sticking their heads out of the washing machine, which they decided to explore one day when the lid was up. Luckily, it didn't have water in it at the time.

Ironing boards are unstable. Put them away when you're through ironing, and don't leave a hot iron unattended.

• In the garage. Put antifreeze, weed killers, pesticides, rodenticides, herbicides, paint, turpentine, dried-up paint rollers, and anything else potentially dangerous in locked cabinets. Wipe up spills immediately.

Automatic garage doors can be dangerous, too. Cats have been known to get caught beneath them. Make sure your cat is under control or out of the garage any time you open or close the door.

Cats like to curl up inside warm car engines for a nap. They get killed when an unsuspecting owner starts the car. If your cat has access to the garage, always bang on the hood of the car to make sure he's not in there before you turn the key in the ignition.

• Throughout the house. Kittens and cats like small, dark, warm, enclosed places. Look for and block off any nooks, crannies, or holes inside cabinetry or behind washer/dryer units. Check beneath the recliner before you put the footrest down, or kitty could get trapped behind it. Make sure you haven't closed your kitten inside a closet or dresser drawer and that all heating and air vents have covers. If you live in a highrise, keep windows screened and balconies off limits. Cats don't have good depth perception, and they apparently don't realize they're jumping six stories instead of six feet.

HE ATE WHAT?!

What are some of the dangerous things my kitten might eat?

Anything small that will fit in a kitten or cat's mouth has the potential to be swallowed and cause problems. Balloons, cigarette butts, coins, dental floss, earrings, nails, needles, pins, paper clips, pills, plastic ties used to bind newspapers, rubber bands, string, thread, twist ties, and yarn can all cause choking, poisoning (pills and pennies), or intestinal obstructions that require surgery to correct. Before you bring your kitten home, go through your home, top to bottom, picking up and putting away these items. Keep them inside drawers or behind cabinet doors secured with child locks. Close sewing kits and put them out of reach.

HOUSEHOLD POISONS

What other household items should I be concerned about?

While your cat might not seek out and drink poisonous substances, it's all too easy for him to ingest them accidentally. Ammonia, bleach, cleaning agents, disinfectants, drain cleaner, gasoline, oven cleaner, paint, and rodent poisons can all kill your cat. How? Let's say that you mop the floor with a pine-scented cleaner and your cat walks on it while it's still damp. He then licks his paws to clean them, ingesting the cleanser. Any time you use cleansers or other chemicals, put your cat in a safe place first and thoroughly wipe up any residue.

POISONOUS PLANTS

I have lots of houseplants. Are there any my kitten shouldn't eat?

Cats do love to nibble on greens, but many house and yard plants are poisonous if eaten. In this chapter, you'll find lists of toxic and nontoxic plants. These lists are not complete, but they include some of the most common plants found in homes and yards. For more information on plants that can be toxic to cats, see the *Cat Owner's Home Veterinary Handbook* (see Appendix III) or visit the Web site of the ASPCA's National Animal Poison Control Center at www.aspca.org.

POISONOUS PLANTS, TAKE TWO

What are the signs of plant toxicity?

That depends on the plant. Some cause rashes or irritation after contact with the mouth or skin. These include chrysanthemum, creeping fig, poinsettia, and weeping fig (*Ficus benjamina*).

Plants that contain oxalic acid can cause swelling in the mouth or sometimes staggering and collapse. Examples are Boston ivy, caladium, calla lily, dumbcane, elephant's ear, mother-in-law plant, and pothos.

Others produce such signs as vomiting, diarrhea, abdominal pain, or cramps. Tremors, respiratory problems, staggering, convulsions, and collapse are also possible signs of plant toxicity. Plants that might cause these signs include amaryllis, asparagus fern, azalea, daffodil, delphinium, English holly, foxglove, ivy, Jerusalem cherry, larkspur, spider mum, umbrella plant, wisteria, and yew.

Sometimes only certain parts of a plant are poisonous, such as the leaves or berries. In others, the entire plant is poisonous. Don't take any risks. If you know a plant is toxic, get rid of it or replace it with a silk version. Remember that the lists here are not complete, and check all of your plants against the other sources I've recommended.

ABOUT ANTIFREEZE

I understand that antifreeze is toxic to cats. Why would cats drink it in the first place?

Antifreeze has a sweet flavor that cats (and dogs) like. Cats can also ingest antifreeze if they walk through it and then lick their paws to clean them. Even very small amounts of antifreeze can be fatal. Antifreeze made of propylene glycol is touted as being less toxic, "less" being the operative word. It's still toxic if your cat ingests enough of it, so don't rely on it to keep your cat safe.

SUSPECTED ANTIFREEZE POISONING

I noticed a small puddle of antifreeze on the garage floor and I know my cat was in there recently. What should I do?

Any time you suspect that your cat has come in contact with antifreeze, take her to the veterinarian immediately. Signs of antifreeze poisoning, which occur in the first few hours after ingestion, are staggering, scizures, extreme thirst, excessive urination, and vomiting. Without treatment, kidney failure sets in and the cat will die.

Antifreeze poisoning is diagnosed with blood and urine tests. Treatment needs to start right away for the cat to have any chance of survival. If you think your cat may have lapped up antifreeze, don't wait for signs to develop—get her to the veterinarian. In cases where the cat is known to have ingested the antifreeze recently, the veterinarian can administer a drug that will prevent the liver from converting antifreeze to its toxic components. This drug is not effective if the cat is already showing signs of poisoning. If it has been a few hours since the cat ingested the antifreeze, the veterinarian will induce vomiting to remove any antifreeze still in the stomach. Charcoal tablets given orally (by mouth) help bind antifreeze in the intestine, preventing it from being broken down by the liver. Take the following steps to help prevent antifreeze poisoning:

- Keep new and used antifreeze in a sealed, leakproof container.
- Take antifreeze to a service station for disposal rather than pouring it on the ground.
- Check your driveway and garage floor for puddles of antifreeze that may have leaked from the car and wipe them up.
- If you pour antifreeze in your toilet (to keep pipes from freezing, for instance), make sure the lid is kept down and the door to the bathroom is closed.

OUTDOOR FUN

Is it all right for my cat to play in my yard?

If you let your cat outdoors—preferably on a supervised basis—you'll need to kitten-proof it as well. For instance, if you treat your lawn with chemicals, you shouldn't let your cat walk on the grass. She could lick the chemicals off her paws and become poisoned. And get rid of any rat poison or snail bait in the yard.

If you have a hot tub or swimming pool, keep it covered. Kittens can fall in and not be able to get out.

The same cautions for houseplants apply to plants in your yard. Bulbs are toxic to cats, as are holly and oleander, which are common outdoor shrubs. Check the toxic plant list for others. Get rid of what you can or don't let your cat roam the yard freely. You may want to build her an enclosure where she can climb, roll in the grass, and lie in the sun, without being exposed to poisonous plants or predators such as coyotes. The Cat Fence-In® containment system is a sturdy effective way to keep your cat safely inside an already fenced yard.

HOLIDAY HAZARDS

I've heard that cats like to climb Christmas trees. What's a good way to prevent this?

Yes, cats are definitely intrigued by the idea of having their very own tree to climb in the house. At least until your cat outgrows kitten antics, you have a few options, none of which are perfect.

The first is to not have a tree. The second is to keep the cat out of the room the tree is in. The third is to surround the tree with some kind of barrier to prevent kitty access. An x-pen (short for exercise pen) from the pet store may work, depending on how athletic and determined your cat is to reach the tree. An x-pen is made of galvanized steel, and comes in various heights and lengths. It looks like a small chain-link fence and can be placed in front of or around areas that you want to block off (assuming that there's no piece of furniture that your cat can use as a launching pad to go over the barrier). You can also use an x-pen—a tall one—to block the door to the room with the tree, although some cats will climb or jump over any barrier.

HOLIDAY HAZARDS, PART TWO

Are there any other holiday or seasonal hazards I should be aware of?

In just about every month of the year, there is some holiday or weather condition that has the potential to affect your cat. Let's go through the calendar and see what you might need to think about as far as kitten- or cat-proofing your home.

January. The new year brings loud and raucous parties, fireworks, and noisemakers, all of which can be stressful to your cat if she's not used to that level of activity or noise. Make some time to spend with her before you have a party or go out. If you're having people over, consider confining her to a quiet room where she won't be disturbed. On the other hand, if she's a social butterfly and knows most of the people who are coming over, there's no reason why she can't make an appearance. Just keep her well away from the roast, pâté, chocolate, and champagne. Cats are sneaky. I still remember the dinner party where my cats hopped up on the kitchen counter to help themselves to the pork roast. Luckily, we had already eaten. Speaking of guests, warn yours not to hand out any treats of any kind, no matter how pitifully your cat meows; you don't want kitty to wake up the next morning with an upset tummy or a hangover.

February through April. For most of us, Valentine's Day and Easter mean chocolate—and lots of it. It's not so great for cats, though. We most commonly hear about chocolate being toxic to dogs, but it can affect cats as well. The toxic (to pets, anyway) element in chocolate is a chemical called theobromine, which stimulates the central nervous system and the cardiovascular system, increases blood pressure, and causes nausea and vomiting. The most dangerous form of chocolate is unsweetened baking chocolate, because it's not adulterated with sugar. Semisweet and milk chocolate contain less theobromine, but they can still cause problems. Keep chocolate out of reach of your cat.

July through September. Fireworks, cookouts, and hot weather mark Independence Day and Labor Day. For both holidays, keep your cat out of the deviled eggs, hamburgers, and other goodies. When dusk falls on the Fourth of July, be sure your cat is indoors. The noise and glare from fireworks can frighten cats. Every fifth of July, shelters take in numerous animals that ran away from home at the first snap, crackle, and pop of the Roman candles, cherry bombs, and sparklers. Don't let your cat be an Independence Day statistic.

If your cat is indoors but still seems frightened by the noise, turn on the television or some music to help drown out the sound. Pull out one of her favorite toys to help distract her.

Summer also brings lightning and thunderstorms in many parts of the country. Some cats are as sensitive to thunder and lightning as they are to fireworks. Use the same distraction techniques described above.

In hot weather, be sure your cat always has fresh water and a cool place to nap, particularly if you don't have air-conditioning. This is especially important for cats with pushed-in faces, such as Persians. Cats can suffer heatstroke and dehydration in extreme temperatures, so be aware of the signs:

- panting
- respiratory distress
- dark red gums
- lethargy
- high body temperature (104 degrees Fahrenheit or more)

Help your cat stay cool in the dog days of summer by keeping him indoors and offering him a frozen towel or a bag of frozen peas to snuggle up with.

Cats that enjoy sunbathing in their custom outdoor kitty enclosures can get sunburned, believe it or not. Sunburn is most common in white cats or cats with white ears or faces. Protect light-haired cats by applying a nontoxic sunscreen recommended by your veterinarian on their ears and nose. Keep hairless cats out of the sun altogether.

October. Black cats, goblins, and witches roam the streets on Halloween in search of sweet treats. Be sure your cat doesn't slip through the open door when you're handing out goodies. To be on the safe side, consider confining her to an interior room so she can't escape. And keep all that candy out of reach. Although it's rare, some cats have a sweet tooth.

November. Like most of our holidays, Thanksgiving centers on food. Your cat will want to partake of the turkey and dressing (or at least the turkey), but rich food isn't good for her. Limit her to a small bite or two of breast meat (dark meat is higher in fat) and forego the gravy and dressing.

This is also the time of year when many of us like to light a fire in the fireplace. If your cat likes to snooze on the warm hearth—and what cat doesn't?—protect him from flying sparks by putting up a fire screen.

December. The previous warnings about food and Christmas trees apply. Other things to keep out of reach are holly, mistletoe, and Christmas tinsel. The chemicals you place in the water of the tree stand are toxic, so don't let your cat drink out of it.

DESIGNING A SAFE OUTDOOR AREA FOR YOUR CAT

It's great fun for cats to go outdoors. There are butterflies to chase and birds to stalk, grass to eat, and sunny spots for cat naps. But the outdoors holds a lot of dangers for cats that are allowed to roam freely: cars, coyotes, diseases, parasites. You can offer a compromise, though, by building your cat an outdoor enclosure where he can safely interact with the environment. Bob Walker, author of *The Cat's House* and owner of eleven cats, offers tips on what might be included in the perfect kitty getaway.

Tip number one is to give cats as much space as possible. That's vertical and horizontal space. Remember that cats like to climb and plan accordingly. Ideally, your structure should be at least six feet by six feet, with a climbing tree, perches at various heights, or high-level walkways (about 5.5 inches wide) that not only hug the walls but that also cross the space diagonally. (A catwalk that only lines the perimeter of a wall doesn't allow the cat any way to turn around.) "Cats love to look down on us," Walker says, "and we find the usage of walkways is greatest where they can show us how adroit and clever they are."

Use tough materials. Screening should be strong enough that neither cat nor a hungry predator can claw through it. The same goes for flooring. It shouldn't be something that other animals could dig beneath to get into the enclosure. A sealed concrete floor is best, Walker says, because it's strong and it can be hosed down as needed. If you're going all out, lay a concrete base that slopes to a drain for easy cleanup. Prevent territorial disputes with wandering cats by building a solid base wall about three feet high. Then have your screening go up from that surface. That helps prevent germs from spreading as well as altercations at screen level.

Your kitty enclosure should have a cover to prevent escape and to provide shelter from the elements. Design the cover so that the enclosure has both shaded and sunny areas. "Cats love to flake out and absorb the rays, but you also need to make sure they don't get fried," Walker says.

A cat door is a good way for your cat to go in and out of the enclosure, but there should be easy access to it for you as well. In case your cat is sick or hurt, you don't want him to be out of reach. You'll probably want to put a litter box in the enclosure, so you'll also need easy access to scoop and change the litter.

Put in planters that contain catnip or other cat-safe plants. See the boxed information at the end of this chapter for plant suggestions.

Many cats enjoy running water. Consider putting in a small fountain that your cat can drink out of or play in, batting at the water with his paws. Water-loving cats such as the Turkish Van may appreciate a small plastic pool or tub that they can splash around in. "I'm designing mine so there's a little running brook," Walker says. Even if you don't go that far, your cat's enclosure should be supplied with fresh drinking water daily.

Try to make the enclosure an area that you'll also enjoy using. Sitting outside, enjoying the outdoors, is a great way to spend time with your cat.

NONTOXIC PLANTS

Listed below are just a few of the plants that are considered to be nontoxic to cats. That doesn't mean your cat won't vomit or have diarrhea if he nibbles on them. It simply means that the cat's reaction to eating the plant is usually mild and doesn't require treatment.

African violet	Crepe myrtle
American rubber plant	Dwarf palm
Baby tears	Garden marigold
Bachelor's buttons	Gloxinia
Bamboo	Grape ivy
Begonia species	Ice plant
Blushing bromeliad	Jasmine
Boston fern	Rose
Camellia	Spider plant
Cat ear	Swedish ivy
Catnip	Umbrella plant
Common snapdragon	Zebra plant
Creeping Charlie	

TOXIC PLANTS

Aloe	Hydrangea
Amaryllis	Iris
Avocado	Jerusalem cherry
Boston ivy	Kalanchoe
Caladium	Lily of the valley
Chinaberry tree	Mistletoe
Cyclamen	Morning glory
Daffodil	Mother-in-law plant
Dieffenbachia	Oleander
Dracaena	Philodendron
Elephant's ear	Pothos
English ivy	Sago palm
Holly	Schefflera
Hyacinth	Yew

CHAPTER 6

Starting Life with Your New Cat

NOW THAT YOU have all your supplies, it's finally time to bring your kitten or cat home and start building a relationship with her. This is a momentous event, one that deserves as much planning and care as you took in the search to find the cat A "getting-to-know-you" period is essential to starting off on the right paw with your cat. You'll both need time to learn each other's ways and rules.

Another consideration is the age of your new cat. Both kittens and older cats will need an adjustment period. Because kittens are young and resilient, without a lot of psychological baggage, they can adapt quickly to new homes. Older cats may need a little more time to learn to trust you and accept a new environment. Be patient, and give them their space. Attention and playtime are fine, but if your cat prefers to sit back and observe for a while, respect her decision.

Whether you're bringing home a kitten or adult cat, take things slow. Don't overwhelm the animal with a lot of new people all at once. The kids' friends or the neighbors may be clamoring to see your new companion, but limit the number of people and amount of petting the cat encounters at any one time. Cats can easily become overstimulated by attention or petting and will respond by scratching or biting.

Make sure the cat has a place she can call her own. If she settles on a favorite sleeping or viewing perch, explain to the kids that they need to respect her privacy when she's there. No teasing her or trying to get her to play if she's not interested. The same goes for her dining area. Teach your children not to bother the cat while she's eating. Cats are like the French: meals are very important to them, and they want to savor the experience without interruptions.

Your kitten will probably need to use the litter box after the car ride to his new home. When you arrive, take him directly to the litter box and place him inside it. By introducing the kitten to the litter box first, you can help prevent accidents in the house. See chapter 13 for more information on litter-box training your cat.

You may want to start out by introducing your cat to only one room in the house, a safe place that she can retreat to if she feels overwhelmed. This safe place can be a bedroom, office, or even a large bathroom. Put a litter box, bed, food and water, and a scratching post in the room, and let the cat fully explore the area. Once she's comfortable there, she can venture out into the rest of the house. It's very important that the safe room has a litter box. You don't want your cat to seek out unauthorized areas to use for elimination.

If you're away from home, confine your cat to the safe room, at least for the first two weeks. She'll feel more secure, and you can control what she can and can't scratch. There's also the reinforcement of the scratching post being the only scratchable item in the room. Otherwise, your cat will simply learn that she can scratch the sofa when you're gone, but not when you're home. After two weeks, a cat's habits are usually established and she's unlikely to vary from them, so make both your lives easier by teaching her what you want from the start.

Whether you've brought home a kitten or an older cat, it's a good idea to get her used to short periods of your absence right away. While it's often not recognized, cats can develop separation anxiety, so they need to learn from the first that you'll always come back. Start by leaving her on her own in a room for a few minutes and build on this until she learns that there are times when she's alone or that you aren't going to give her attention. Another way to lessen the chance that your cat will become anxious in your absence is to reduce the amount of attention you give her just before you leave. When you return, greet her calmly instead of making a big fuss over her. She'll learn that departures and arrivals aren't anything to worry about.

CAR TRAVEL

What's the best way to bring your new cat home? The kids want to hold him in the car, but that doesn't seem very safe.

You're right; having a loose kitten or cat in the car isn't the greatest idea. Explain to the kids that just as they wear seat belts or ride in car seats to stay safe, the cat needs to ride in his carrier so he won't be harmed in case of a sudden stop or accident. You can place the carrier between them in the back seat so they can still see and talk to the cat on the ride home.

MOTION COMMOTION

Do cats get car sick?

Like people, some cats get car sick, some don't. If you're concerned that your new cat might have an upset stomach and throw up on the ride home, line his carrier with a towel, which will add to his comfort and be easy to throw in the washing machine after you get home.

If you know that your cat gets car sick, withhold food before a car trip, or feed him dry food, which is less likely to cause stomach upset than canned food. You may also want to try giving the cat Rescue Remedy, a Bach Original Flower Essence that has calming properties, before the ride. Look for it at health food stores.

BED TIME

Where should my kitten sleep at night?

Your kitten or cat will probably make that choice for himself, unless you confine him to a specific area. While a cat may use a cuddle bed on the floor for naps during the day, he won't necessarily sleep in it at night. You can leave beds in places where your cat prefers to sleep, but be prepared for him to hop on the bed with you.

PET THE CAT

My children are very young. How can I teach them to pet and hold the cat nicely?

One of the best lessons you can teach young children is how to properly approach and pet an animal. It will stand them in good stead throughout their lives.

Show a child by example how to stroke the cat gently. Hold her hand as she moves it over the cat's body. Try teaching the "three-finger rule"—that is, the cat can only be petted or touched with three fingers. Children like to imitate, and yours will follow your lead if you show them how to pet the cat.

Offer frequent reminders not only to stroke softly but also to speak softly. Cats have very sensitive ears. Point out how much the cat likes it when the child pets him quietly and calmly. Repeatedly stress that your child must be gentle with the cat: no kicking, hitting, squeezing, or tail pulling allowed—ever. You never want the cat to feel that he must scratch or bite to protect himself from the child.

Appeal to the child's sense of empathy. If she pushes the cat, ask if she would like being pushed that way. When she says "No," explain that the cat doesn't like it either. You'll probably have this discussion over and over again until your child reaches the age of reason.

It's best to supervise all interactions a toddler has with the cat. If you can't be there to keep an eye on things, the cat or the child should be in a safe place so the two of them can't interact. Every time you see your child reach for the cat, remind her that she can only pet him when you're there to "help."

A good rule to establish is that young children (below the age of six years) can only hold the cat when they're sitting on the ground. No picking the kitten or cat up and hauling him around like a rag doll. It's not comfortable for the cat, and he runs the risk of being injured if the child accidentally drops him.

Be aware that toddlers go through a stage of being rough or aggressive toward animals. They're not yet old enough to understand that their actions toward the cat are hurtful. Just because this behavior is normal, though, doesn't mean you should allow it. Set boundaries and consistently reinforce the message that your child must interact nicely with the cat or there will be consequences. Some parents restrict access to the cat (much to the cat's relief, no doubt), give the child a time-out, or take away a favorite toy or privilege. And make sure the cat always has a way to escape a child's attentions, such as a tall cat tree he can climb or a baby gate raised about six inches off the floor. This leaves plenty of room for a cat to slip underneath while still keeping the child safe.

If your cat doesn't enjoy being petted by children, no matter how nice they are, there are other positive ways they can interact. Suggest that the child draw a picture of the cat, or help her bake cat treats for him. Having a child pull a fishing pole or feather toy for the cat to chase can keep cat and child amused for hours.

A good way to introduce young children to pet care is to let them take care of their stuffed animals while you take care of the real cat. They can pretend to give the stuffed animal food and water or stroke the stuffed animal with a soft brush while you groom your cat.

Teach your child how to pet the cat nicely, and always supervise when they're together.

PICK UP LINES

How should I pick up my cat?

That's easy. Place one hand behind the front legs and another beneath the hindquarters. Lift gently. Mother cats carry their kittens by the scruff of the neck, but you can injure a cat by doing that yourself.

COSTUME PARTY

My kids want to dress up the kitten and wheel her around in a baby buggy. Is this a good way for them to play together?

That all depends on the cat. Some cats are perfectly amenable to playing dress up and will tolerate this game for long periods, simply walking away when they're tired of it. Others are less patient and may resort to scratching or biting to get away. If your cat has a laid-back personality and doesn't seem to object to wearing a bonnet and riding in a baby buggy, then I don't see any problem with permitting it. Be careful with costumes that could injure the cat if his paws get caught in them. Keep an eye on things and put an end to the play session if the cat wants to get away. Teach your kids that if the cat runs off, they're not to drag her back for more.

CATS VERSUS DOGS

What's the best way to introduce our new cat to the dog?

Contrary to popular opinion, cats and dogs can get along just fine and have even been known to become the best of friends. That doesn't happen automatically, though. You need to take some precautions when introducing them so that they learn respect for each other.

Put your dog on a leash before you bring the cat in. A rambunctious puppy may try to lunge at a cat—especially if he's never encountered one before—and might receive a painful swat on the nose for his pains. Say "No" and restrain the puppy with the leash if he goes for the cat or tries to play too roughly with her. Reward him with praise and a treat if he ignores the cat or tries to sniff her gently.

The best way to introduce a cat and dog is to have one or the other in a crate the first time they meet. That way they can see and smell each other before any physical get-together takes place. Expect some hissing on the cat's part and curious sniffing from the dog. A good time for a cage-free meeting is when both animals are relaxed or even a little tired.

If your cat stands her ground and lets the dog know who's in charge, they'll likely get along well. A cat that runs, however, may stimulate the dog's prey drive, and their interactions will need close supervision until the dog learns that the cat is off limits. Be aware that some breeds such as Siberian huskies, terriers, and sight hounds (grey-hounds, salukis, and whippets, for instance) have a strong hunting instinct and will instinctively chase a running cat, seriously injuring or even killing her if they're not restrained. You may need to keep them in separate areas if the dog can't be retrained or controlled.

CATNAPS

My cat sure seems to sleep a lot. Is this normal?

Well, we don't know why, but it is perfectly normal for a cat to sleep up to eighteen hours a day. Kittens and old cats sleep the most, but any cat will settle down for a nice catnap after a good meal or a game of pounce on the mouse. If you see your cat's paws twitching or his tail swishing while he's asleep, he's probably dreaming about finally catching that bird he sees out the window every day.

SOME LIKE IT HOT

Why do cats like warm spots?

A cat's desire for warmth harks back to kittenhood, when he found warmth and nourishment while nursing. Warmth also just plain feels good. Heat helps soothe arthritic joints, for instance.

Some cats will do anything for the heat they crave, from the dangerous—lying on a gas heater—to the innocuous—napping in a pool of sunshine. Provide your cat with a cozy bed where he can cuddle or buy or build a window perch to place in that perfect sunny spot.

THE MIGHTY HUNTER

*My cat is always bringing me dead birds and mice. What am I
supposed to do with them?*

Cats are superb predators, and part of their hunting instinct is to
bring their take to a safe place where it can be eaten. Where better
than their own home? Before we started keeping them indoors, our
first two cats used to bring prey straight to their food dishes. Other
than the ick factor, I always thought it was pretty smart of them to
make that association. Praise your cat for her hunting prowess and
try to distract her while you or your spouse dispose of her prize.
Keeping your cat indoors is the best way to prevent this behavior, although indoor cats have been known to substitute stuffed animals or
other toys for prey and will bring them to you meowing loudly and
proudly. An indoor cat is also less likely to incur injuries or contract
diseases.

TERRITORIAL MARKER

Why does my cat rub up against me?

Cats are territorial animals who use scent to make a place their own.
Urine and feces contain scent markers, as do the sebaceous glands,
which secrete sebum, a thick, semifluid substance made up of fat and
cellular debris. The sebaceous glands, which are attached to hair fol-
licles, are largest and most numerous in the areas a cat commonly
uses to mark his territory: the lips, chin, base of the tail, and scrotum.
In addition to their function of protecting the coat, the sebaceous
glands help the cat identify his environment. When he rubs his face
against your leg or a piece of furniture, he's marking the area as his
own. Be pleased that your cat considers you his property.

THE NAMING OF CATS

In his poem "The Naming of Cats," T. S. Eliot tells us that

> "a cat needs a name that's particular, A name that's peculiar, and more dignified, Else how can he keep up his tail perpendicular, Or spread out his whiskers, or cherish his pride?"

Clearly, there are rules when it comes to naming a cat. You want something that sounds good, that's easy to call out, and that suits the cat's personality. Choose a name that will place your cat in a positive light, even if she seems to be a troublemaker by nature. I can tell you from experience that I've regretted the times I've named a cat Trouble or Pandora. Even if they don't know what it means, cats will live up—or down—to a name because of the associations you make with it, however innocently or humorously.

The ideal name is only one or two syllables or can easily be shortened. Cats can be named for favorite places or the city or state where you acquired them; for favorite flowers, foods, or drinks; or for their color or personality. Plays on words are always fun, too. We named our gray cat Peter the Gray (a TV miniseries on Peter the Great was popular at the time). Consider the time of year. At age five, I named my first cat Mr. Boo, because he was solid black and we got him at Halloween.

Don't be in a hurry to name your cat. Give him time, and he'll likely tell you himself what it should be. The following suggestions will help you choose the perfect name for your cat.

Amber, Cinnamon, Ginger, Godiva, Hershey, Nutmeg, Spice: for red, orange, or brown cats

Aria, Figaro, Jazz, Mozart, Sonata: for cats belonging to music lovers

Bagheera, Butch Catsidy, Cat Ballou, Felix, Sylvester, The Great Catsby, Tigger: cat-related cartoon or movie names

Boise, Cleveland, Florida, Jamaica, Paris, Purrsia: place names

Boris, Natasha: for a Russian Blue or Siberian cat

Cashmere, Catillac, Champagne, Chanel, Dior, Satin, Silk: for plush or expensive cats

Colette, Hemingway: for a writer's cat

Columbus, Drake, Magellan: for a cat that likes to explore

Countess, Duchess, Jezebel, Napoleon, Pharaoh, Princess: for the cat that rules with an iron paw

Daffodil, Holly, Iris, Jasmine, Magnolia, Primrose, Violet: after favorite flowers, trees, or plants

Earl Gray, Fog: for gray cats

Evinrude: for a cat that purrs loudly

Fillmore: for a cat that likes to eat

Fireball, Fracas: for a cat that causes a ruckus

Garbo: for a cat that keeps to herself

Gin and Tonic: for a pair of cats

Hestia (goddess of the hearth in Greek mythology): for a cat that likes to lie by the fire

Inkspot, Indigo: for black cats

Jitterbug, Xena: for an active cat

Kahlua, Martini, Whiskey: after favorite beverages

Karma: for a cat acquired by fate

Valentine, Venus: for a loving cat

Wizard: for a cat that's good at disappearing

Whisper, Whispurr: for a quiet cat

Some other good cat names: Abby, Daphne, Inca, India, Isabel, Leo, Lulu, Muffin

CHAPTER 7

Your New Cat's Health Issues

I F YOU HAVE just acquired your cat, whether she's a kitten or an adult, or if you have moved recently, finding a good veterinarian should be at the top of your to-do list. The relationship you build with your veterinarian, as well as his or her relationship with your cat, can make a big difference in your cat's health over the years. It's important not only to be confident in a veterinarian's abilities, but also for your cat to be comfortable in his or her care.

Word of mouth is probably the most common method of finding a veterinarian. Ask friends, neighbors, or coworkers if they like their veterinarians, why they use them, what they like about the hospital, and even what they don't like. If you purchased your kitten from a breeder, he may be able to recommend someone in your area. If you are moving to a new town, ask your former veterinarian if he or she can recommend a colleague in the new locale.

Another good place to search is in the Yellow Pages of your phone directory. An advertisement can tell you how long a veterinarian has been in practice, whether the clinic offers boarding or grooming services, and if any specialists are on staff. It's also a good way to locate clinics near your home.

When you have the names of a few veterinarians, set up an appointment to meet the veterinarians and tour their hospitals. It's a good idea to interview several veterinarians to make sure you have the same health-care philosophy. The hospital tour and a meeting with the veterinarian and the staff will help you make a good decision. Remember, not every hospital—even if it's a good one—is going to suit everyone. It's important to find a hospital that suits your needs, provides the level of care you want, has the attitude you want in the lay staff, and has a veterinarian who provides what you're looking for. You may prefer a veterinarian who's chatty or has a fatherly or motherly manner, while your neighbor may look for someone who has a more formal or academic approach. It's all a matter of personal taste. If you aren't comfortable with a veterinarian's manner toward clients or animals, try someplace else.

Note whether the veterinarian answers your questions readily and clearly. A good veterinarian is a good communicator. Brief, mumbled answers without any details don't inspire confidence. And you should be able to understand what the veterinarian tells you without having to work through a lot of $10 veterinary terms. Avoid a veterinarian who makes you feel either ignorant or demanding.

The staff, too, should communicate clearly and courteously. Do they answer the telephone promptly and greet clients in a friendly manner? Do the veterinarian and staff have a good rapport with the animals they treat?

What you look for in a veterinary clinic can also depend on other factors that are important to you. Do you want a high-tech clinic or a family practice? Can you get referrals for specialty care if needed? Emergency coverage is a biggie. Ask the doctors their philosophy on things that are important to you. Such things might include how the veterinarian feels about raw or homemade diets or the administration and frequency of vaccinations.

Consider, too, whether the veterinarian is affiliated with a professional organization, such as the American Animal Hospital Association (AAHA) or a holistic or homeopathic veterinary medical association. Such organizations usually have a set of standards that veterinarians must meet to maintain their membership, and some, such as the AAHA, inspect the hospital and staff to ensure that standards are being met. Membership in AAHA isn't automatically a sign that a clinic is well run, but it does indicate that the hospital has met certain standards established by AAHA.

You may want a veterinarian who specializes in cats. Ask if he or she is a member of the American Association of Feline Practitioners (AAFP) or is certified in feline practice by the American Board of Veterinary Practitioners.

To find veterinarians with a natural bent, visit www.altvetmed.com. It lists the directories of a number of associations for complementary and alternative veterinary medicine, including the Academy of Veterinary Homeopathy, the American Academy of Veterinary Acupuncture, the American Holistic Veterinary Medical Association, the American Veterinary Chiropractic Association, and the International Veterinary Acupuncture Society.

Once you find a veterinarian you like, make an appointment to bring your cat in for an examination. Even if the cat is up to date on vaccinations, it's a good idea for the veterinarian to see your cat when she's healthy, so he can have a baseline against which to judge her health.

Ideally, a first visit doesn't involve any painful or invasive procedures, such as vaccinations. Schedule something simple, such as a toenail trim or a dental exam. Also, if you're new to the vicinity, the veterinarian can advise you about concerns specific to cat owners there. For instance, outdoor cats in Florida can have run-ins with the Bufo toad, which secretes a poisonous substance through its skin. Cats that go outdoors in the western United States, especially in New Mexico, Arizona, Colorado, and Utah, run the risk of contracting the plague, transmitted when the cat eats an infected rodent or is bitten by a flea from an infected rodent. (All the more reason to keep your cat indoors!)

This type of information and interaction is invaluable. In the best of all worlds, your cat will see the same veterinarian for her entire life. The relationship the three of you build should have a foundation of trust and communication. The following questions and answers will help you be prepared for the various health-related situations you may encounter with your new cat.

QUESTIONS TO ASK

What are some of the questions I should ask when I'm selecting a veterinary clinic?

Before you visit a clinic, get on the phone and get the answers to the following questions:

- What percentage of your clinic's patients are cats? (If you have a pedigreed cat, ask if they see any other cats of your particular breed.)
- What are your office hours?
- How do you handle after-hours emergencies? Ideally, they're affiliated with a nearby animal emergency center.
- Do you provide twenty-four-hour coverage for hospitalized animals? (If they don't, ask how overnight patients are monitored.)
- What are your fees for office visits, spay/neuter surgery, and vaccinations?
- What forms of payment do you accept?

- Does the veterinarian make house calls? Under what circumstances?
- Who fills in when the veterinarian isn't available?

WHY SPAY AND NEUTER?

I don't want to subject my cat to unnecessary surgery. Why does my cat need to be spayed or neutered?

Spaying and neutering has a number of health benefits for cats and societal benefits for people. Spaying, especially before a cat's first heat, reduces or prevents such health problems as mammary tumors (breast cancer), uterine cancer, and pyometra, a potentially fatal uterine infection. In males, neutering reduces the risk of testicular cancer, enlargement of the prostate, and related infections. And a Winn Feline Foundation study found that, contrary to popular opinion, neutered animals were just as active as their unaltered age mates, so weight gain can't be blamed on spay or neuter surgery.

People benefit because spayed or neutered animals are less aggressive, more affectionate, and less likely to wander or fight. Society benefits because fewer cats reproduce, leading to fewer homeless cats. That not only saves a community money, it also eases the burden on shelter workers who must perform the sad task of euthanasia.

EARLY SPAY/NEUTER SURGERY

I thought cats had to be at least six months old before they could get spayed or neutered, but my veterinarian says it's being done at a much younger age now. Is this safe?

Conventional wisdom dictates that kittens be spayed or neutered at age six months or older. Some old wives' tales even suggest that female cats be allowed to have a litter before their reproductive organs are removed. But veterinarians and well-informed pet owners now know that spaying animals before they reach sexual maturity can prevent many health and behavior problems. And the six-month rule no longer applies: Veterinarians can safely perform spay/neuter surgeries on kittens as young as six weeks of age. Young kittens are extremely resilient, recovering quickly from a procedure that would physically stress an older kitten or adult cat. Cats that are six months or older may take several days to a week to recuperate from surgery, compared to younger kittens, who are often up and around in a matter of hours. Veterinarians have learned that the procedures are easier to perform on young kittens, taking less time and requiring less anesthesia. Breeders can ensure that kittens sold as pets, or those with genetic or conformation flaws, won't accidentally reproduce. Some buyers are attracted by the convenience of taking home an already-altered kitten. And animal shelters see the procedure as a way of reducing the flow of animals through their doors.

A Winn Feline Foundation study showed no differences in development that could negatively affect a cat. Concerns that early spay/neuter surgery could halt or impair development of the urinary tract, resulting in an increased incidence of cystitis and related problems, turned out to be unfounded. The ongoing study hopes to show that if all animals adopted from shelters are neutered before adoption, there will be a corresponding decrease in the numbers of animals euthanized each year.

KITTEN VACCINATIONS

Why does my kitten need so many vaccinations?

Kittens are born with temporary immunity to disease. They acquire this immunity the first time they nurse, from colostrum, the first milk their mother produces, which contains maternal antibodies against disease. These maternal antibodies provide what is called passive immunity, which helps protect the kitten against infectious diseases until her immune system is strong enough to function on its own.

Passive immunity decreases as the kitten grows and gradually disappears. It's possible, then, for a kitten to have maternal antibodies that aren't numerous enough to fight off disease but that are still able to interfere with the antibodies produced by immunization. It's during this window of opportunity that your kitten is most vulnerable to disease. To counteract this problem, your kitten receives a series of vaccinations, usually beginning at six to eight weeks of age, and repeated at three- or four-week intervals until maternal immunity has disappeared and your kitten's immune system is stimulated, usually by twelve to fourteen weeks of age. The exception is the rabies vaccine, which isn't given until sixteen weeks of age.

VACCINATION UPDATE

I've heard a lot about vaccinations being dangerous and unnecessary for cats. What's the real scoop?

Most of us have been brought up with the idea that vaccinations, although momentarily painful, are a good thing. Certainly that can be true, but the key, as with so many things, is moderation. Many immunologists and veterinarians are coming to believe that the annual vaccinations so many cats receive are unnecessary at best and unhealthy at worst. Here's the latest on whether cats need annual vaccinations and which vaccinations are important.

Vaccinations, or immunizations, work by preparing the body's immune system to fight off particular disease-causing organisms. They do this by triggering what is known as acquired immunity, which provides long-term protection against specific diseases, such as feline distemper (panleukopenia) or feline calicivirus, which causes upper respiratory tract diseases. Immunization involves giving small doses of an antigen—such as weakened live or dead viruses—to activate the immune system's memory. Specialized white blood cells develop that recognize and fight off the antigen the next time it enters the body, preventing infection or reducing the severity of the disease.

The problem with vaccinations in cats is that veterinarians have begun to see an increase in the incidence of cancerous tumors known as sarcomas at commonly used feline vaccine sites, such as between the shoulder blades. The benefits of vaccinations outweigh the risks of tumors, but new vaccination protocols can help reduce the chance that a tumor will develop. It's now recommended that vaccines containing rabies antigen be given in the right rear leg, as far down as possible. Vaccines containing feline leukemia virus antigen should be given in the left rear leg, as far down as possible. That way, if cancer develops, the cat will have a better chance of surviving surgery or amputation. Any other vaccines should be given on the right shoulder.

As to which vaccinations your cat needs, that depends a lot on your cat's lifestyle and environment. If your cat lives indoors and doesn't come in contact with other cats, he probably doesn't need the same vaccinations or the same frequency of vaccinations as a cat that's allowed to roam outdoors. Other factors to consider are the protective ability of the vaccine, the frequency or severity of potential reactions from the vaccine, and the age and health of your cat. Among the vaccines that are available for cats are rabies, feline panleukopenia, feline calicivirus/feline rhinotracheitis, feline leukemia virus, chlamydia, feline infectious peritonitis, and ringworm.

- Rabies. The number of rabies cases reported in cats is more than that in all other domestic animals. Because rabies is fatal and because of the public health aspect (rabies can be transmitted from animals to humans through a bite or scratch), all cats need a rabies vaccine, even if they live indoors. I can tell you from experience that your indoor cat *can* escape, despite all your precautions, and that a rabid bat can fly into your house—a situation that those of us who live in suburbia never expect to encounter but which happened at our house only recently. Most rabies vaccinations are good for at least three years. My aged, indoor cats had not had a rabies vaccination in seven years at the time of the bat incident, but their rabies titers (the concentration of an antibody in blood serum) were still high. A rabies vaccination not only protects your cat from accidental exposure to a rabid animal, it's also required by law in many states.

- Feline panleukopenia. Also known as feline distemper, this is a highly contagious and deadly viral disease. The AAFP recommends this vaccine for all cats on the following schedule: a kitten series, a booster shot at one year of age, followed by a booster shot no more frequently than once every three years.

- Feline calicivirus/feline rhinotracheitis. These two viruses are responsible for the majority of infectious upper respiratory diseases in cats, and most cats are exposed to one or both of these viruses at some time in their lives. The vaccines help prevent or reduce the severity of the disease and are also recommended for all cats by the AAFP, on the same schedule recommended for the panleukopenia vaccine.

- Feline leukemia virus. This disease is the leading viral killer of cats. Cats at risk are those that go outdoors or that live in households with FeLV-infected cats. The AAFP recommends this vaccine only for cats at risk of exposure: that is, cats that are not restricted to an indoor, FeLV-negative home.

- All other vaccines. The AAFP does not recommend the routine use of vaccines for chlamydia, feline infectious peritonitis, bordetella, or giardia. These should be decided on a case by case basis, in consultation with your veterinarian.

VACCINE REACTIONS

I've heard that cats can have reactions to vaccinations. What is a reaction and what are the signs?

Vaccinations are usually safe, but they're not entirely risk-free. A reaction is the body's response to a foreign substance, in this case, an antigen. Common mild reactions include discomfort at the site of the vaccination, a mild fever, reduced appetite or energy level, or a small swelling beneath the skin where the vaccine was given. These reactions usually develop anywhere from a few minutes to a few days after vaccination.

More serious reactions, which are rare, can include anaphylactic shock, a life-threatening allergic reaction, or the development of a sarcoma at the vaccine site. Anaphylaxis usually occurs within several minutes to an hour after vaccination. Sarcomas can develop weeks or months after vaccination.

To reduce the risk of a reaction, vaccinate only healthy kittens or cats. If your cat has ever had a vaccine reaction, remind the veterinarian of it before your cat is vaccinated again so he or she can take precautions.

FELINE ANXIETY

My cat is always so anxious when I take her to the veterinarian. Is there any way I can make the visit more comfortable for her?

If cats had their druthers, they'd simply stay at home. Being taken to a funny-smelling veterinary office filled with other animals is not their idea of a good time. You can, however, take steps to make a clinic visit less stressful and more productive for all concerned.

Some veterinary offices accommodate cats by having separate entrances for them or separate reception areas and exam rooms. Going to a cats-only practice or sitting in a cats-only waiting room can help alleviate the stress that can be created by the presence of dogs.

If the clinic you go to has a mixed practice, position yourself in the waiting room away from other animals. You may also ask the receptionist if there's a time you can come in when no dogs are scheduled. That's not a guarantee—emergencies do happen—but it can reduce the chance of kitty encountering a canine.

It's also a good idea to transport your cat in a carrier. Be sure to allow time at home for your cat to become accustomed to the carrier. Set the carrier out, with the door or top off, and place a towel or other bedding inside it. Your cat can then spend time in and around the carrier, marking it with her chin and claiming it as her own.

Many cats seem to feel more comfortable in soft-sided carriers, and it's easier to lift the cat out of a duffle-style bag. If you have to struggle to get the cat out of the carrier, you've set up a stressful situation before the veterinarian even walks into the exam room.

One thing that can make a veterinary visit easier is use of a product called Feliway, a synthetic collection of facial pheromones, the chemicals cats use to mark territory. Feliway marks any area that's sprayed with it as cat space and has the effect of lowering the cat's anxiety when the cat enters that space. Spray the carrier with Feliway or bring some with you to spray in the exam room.

Cats that are known to be nervous can sometimes benefit from the use of Bach flower remedies. Rescue Remedy or Calming Essence often seem to have a positive effect. Try administering one of them at home, just before you put your cat in the carrier. Once you're in the exam room, you'll probably have a few minutes before the veterinarian arrives. Open the carrier and give your cat an opportunity to come out on his own. Spreading a towel on the exam table can also help. Cats are often more comfortable on a towel than on a hard, cold surface.

Your veterinarian can help soothe the cat as well. "During the first part of a visit, we talk to the owner so the cat isn't the focus of everything," says John Hamil, DVM, of Canyon Animal Hospital in Laguna Beach, California. "We talk to the cat and stroke him so he calms down. Talking to the cat in a low tone of voice is helpful."

Finally, help set the tone of the visit for the cat by remaining calm and relaxed. Your cat is in tune with your body language more than you realize. If you are upset or nervous, your cat will be too.

FAHRENHEIT 101.5

What's a cat's normal body temperature?

A cat's normal body temperature is 101.5 degrees Fahrenheit, with an acceptable variance of one degree higher or lower. If your cat seems unwell but doesn't have any apparent signs of illness, take his temperature. Call your veterinarian if the temperature is below 100 degrees Fahrenheit or if it is 103 degrees Fahrenheit or higher. A high temperature can be symptomatic of an infection or heatstroke. Low body temperature is abnormal as well and can indicate a serious problem.

FEVER FINDER

How do I take my cat's temperature?

The good news is that ear thermometers are now available for use with cats, although they aren't quite as accurate as rectal thermometers. Ear thermometers measure infrared heat emanating from the ear drum. Normal ear temperature in cats ranges from 100 to 103 degrees Fahrenheit. Use an ear thermometer designed for use with cats and place it into the horizontal ear canal to ensure an accurate reading.

The bad news is that if you don't have an ear thermometer, you'll have to take your cat's temperature rectally, using a bulb or digital thermometer. To do this, shake the thermometer (if it's a bulb type) to bring the mercury down below 94 degrees Fahrenheit. Lube it with petroleum jelly, K-Y jelly, or vegetable oil. With the cat lying flat on his side or abdomen—it helps to have an assistant to make sure the cat remains in position—move the tail and gently insert the thermometer an inch to an inch and a half into the cat's rectum, using a slight twisting motion. Don't force the thermometer. Wait until your cat relaxes, and be sure to insert it in the hole closest to the tail. Remove the thermometer after one to three minutes and note the temperature.

GETTING A URINE SAMPLE

The veterinarian wants a urine sample. How do I go about getting it?

Sometimes a urine sample is needed to diagnose a bladder or kidney infection. In most instances it's best if the sample is obtained by the veterinarian, but if for some reason you need to gather it, the following method should work.

Empty and clean the litter box. Rinse it thoroughly to remove any cleanser residue. Place a few thin strips of newspaper inside and wait for the cat to urinate. After urination, tip the box so the urine runs into a corner. You can remove a sample with an eyedropper or a small paper cup. Once you've collected the urine, refrigerate the sample if you're not taking it directly to the veterinarian. Don't wait too long to take it or chemical changes will occur.

GIVING MEDICATION

My cat has to take pills for a week because of an infection. How can I make the pill-giving experience pleasant for both of us? And what if I have to give other types of medications?

Successfully giving medication to a cat is an art, and as with all arts, practice makes perfect. This is a good opportunity for you to become comfortable with pilling your cat, because chances are that you'll have to do it again some time in the cat's life. To give a pill, the first step is to keep the cat still. It's best to enlist a helper. Have someone hold your cat while you give the pill. If no assistance is available, kneel on the floor and firmly hold the cat between your knees with your ankles crossed so the cat can't back out. Alternative ways to immobilize the cat are to wrap her in a towel or to place her in a special bag made just for this purpose. Such bags, which leave only the head sticking out, are available from pet supply stores or catalogs. Sometimes it's easier to place the cat on a table or counter rather than on the floor. Experiment until you find what works best for you.

With the pill in your right hand, gently open the cat's jaws, using the first and third fingers of your left hand to apply gentle pressure to the corners of the mouth. This will cause your cat's mouth to open. (Reverse all of these directions if you're a lefty.) Place the pill far back on the tongue, then close the cat's mouth and stroke her throat to encourage swallowing.

Another technique is to hold the cat's head in your left hand and tip the head back until the cat is looking straight up. Holding the pill between the thumb and forefinger of your right hand, open the mouth with the middle finger of your right hand. Drop the pill into the back of the mouth and push it over the tongue with the index finger of your right hand. While holding the mouth closed, let the head assume a normal position and rub or blow into your cat's nose to make her lick, which induces swallowing.

If you aren't able to give your cat a pill using the above methods, disguise the pill by wrapping it in something tasty: a soft cat treat, cream cheese, liver sausage, or peanut butter. Unless a cat is extremely bright or picky, the pill will go down without a problem. I have to admit that this is my favored method of pill-giving, but you should check first with your veterinarian to make sure it's okay to give the pill with food.

Remember that cats can be tricky. They've been known to hold pills in their mouths and then spit them out when you're not looking. To ensure that medication is effective, it's important to perfect your pill-giving technique so the cat receives the entire amount prescribed at the appropriate time each day. Never stop giving medication until it's all gone, even if the cat appears to be well.

Giving a cat a pill requires cunning, patience, and dexterity.

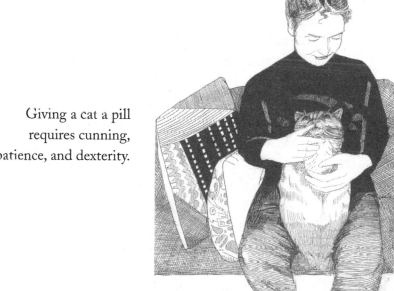

Tips on giving other medications:

- Ear drops. Putting drops into a cat's ears requires skill, because if he shakes his head, most of the medication gets rained all over you. To avoid this, hold the cat between your knees as described above and gently but firmly hold the ear. Tilt the head slightly to the opposite side, and put the required amount in the ear. Then gently fold the ear down and massage the cartilage at the base of the ear. The massaging action gets the medication into the ear, ensuring that less of it is lost when the cat shakes his head. Unless his ears are unusually painful, your cat will probably enjoy this brief massage.

- Eye drops. Prepare the eye dropper before restraining your cat. Holding the dropper in your hand, tilt your cat's head upward and place the drops in the inner corner of the eye, directly over the eyeball. Try not to touch the eye with the tip of the applicator. Distribute the medication evenly by opening and closing the eyelids.
- Liquid medications. Fill a medicine dropper with the appropriate amount of medication. Restrain your cat as described above. Tilting the head upward, open the mouth and aim the eye dropper at the cheek pouch. Holding the mouth closed around the dropper, squeeze out the medication in amounts that aren't too large to be swallowed. The cat's automatic swallowing reflex will kick in as the liquid reaches the back of the mouth. You can also rub or blow on the cat's nose to make him lick, which also initiates the swallowing reflex.
- Ointments. These are usually applied to a cat's eyes or ears. To medicate eyes, hold the cat's head steady and gently pull down on the lower eyelid, exposing the inner eyelid. Apply the ointment to the inside lower lid, being careful to avoid directly touching the eyeball. You may also pull back the upper lid and place the ointment over, not on the white of the eye. After application, close the cat's eyelids to distribute the medication. To apply ointments to ears, follow the above directions for ear drops.

VETERINARY SPECIALISTS

My cat has been diagnosed with a serious heart problem. Is there such a thing as a kitty cardiologist?

Yes, there is. When a cat needs more help than a general-practice veterinarian can provide, you will be referred to a board-certified specialist. Specialists receive extensive postgraduate training in their fields through internships and residencies, which typically last three to four years. Before they can practice a particular specialty, they must pass a credential review and rigorous examinations. Once they meet all the requirements, they are admitted as diplomats of the college for their specialty.

The practice of a board-certified specialist is usually limited to the area of his or her expertise. Veterinarians may specialize in such fields as anesthesiology, behavior, cardiology, dentistry, dermatology, emergency and critical care, feline practice, internal medicine, neurology, nutrition, oncology (cancer), ophthalmology, pathology, radiology, theriogenology (reproduction), surgery, and toxicology.

EEEW! THAT SMELL!

My cat sat on my lap today and when she got up there were a couple of wet spots on my clothes where she'd been, and they smelled awful. What could have caused it?

Like dogs, cats have two anal glands, or sacs, located on each side of the anus. These are scent glands that give the cat's stool an odor that helps the cat mark territory. The anal glands can become impacted if they don't empty properly when the cat defecates, although this isn't as common a problem in cats as it is in dogs. If this becomes a recurring problem in your cat, your veterinarian can show you how to empty the glands yourself—one cat owner does it on a monthly basis—or if you're squeamish you can take your cat to the veterinarian to have this stinky job done—the secretions from the anal sac have been described as smelling a lot like dead fish.

Anal glands can also become infected, indicated by blood or pus in the anal gland secretions, swelling on one or both sides of the anus, or the cat frequently scooting on the ground or carpet or licking the anal area to try to relieve the discomfort he feels. If infections recur, the glands can be removed surgically.

ALLERGIC REACTIONS

I saw my cat get stung by a bee, and the place where she was stung swelled up. For future reference, what should I do in case of a bee sting?

Cats often get stung on a paw because they've been batting at an insect. The swelling from an allergic reaction occurs rapidly. The swelling itself isn't painful, but it can be dangerous if the sting occurs on the head or throat, because the swelling can impede the cat's breathing.

If you know your cat has been stung by a bee, wasp, or other stinging insect, you can help ease the pain by using tweezers to remove the stinger (in the case of a bee) and then applying a paste made with baking soda and water to the affected area. Ice packs can also help relieve swelling and pain. If the area seems to be itchy, apply calamine lotion or Cortaid.

If your cat has a more severe allergic reaction, give him Benadryl at a dose of 1 mg per pound of body weight and take the cat to the veterinarian immediately.

RESPIRATORY WORRIES

My cat is sneezing and her eyes are runny. Does she have a cold?

Cats are prone to respiratory viruses, of which feline viral rhinotracheitis and feline calicivirus are the best known. Signs of respiratory viral disease include a watery or puslike discharge from the eyes and nose, lots of sneezing, and ulcers in the mouth and on the nose. Cats with respiratory viruses can go on to develop pneumonia and secondary bacterial infections, as well as a fever. These viruses spread quickly, so if you have more than one cat, take the sick one to the veterinarian as soon as possible and isolate him from the other cats.

Viruses don't respond to antibiotics, although your veterinarian may prescribe them to prevent bacterial infections from taking hold. Your cat will also need home care to treat his symptoms. Clean his eyes and nose regularly throughout the day with cotton balls or a clean washcloth dampened with warm water. Throw the cotton balls away and clean the washcloth with hot water after every use. A cool-air vaporizer can help the cat breathe more easily. You can achieve the same effect by taking the cat in the bathroom while you shower (don't turn on the exhaust fan). It's also important to encourage your cat to eat. His sense of smell will be dulled, so clean his nose before meals and warm his food to enhance the aroma.

WHEN TO VISIT THE VETERINARIAN

Every cat should be examined annually by a veterinarian. Even if you choose not to vaccinate your cat every year, she still needs a physical exam to make sure her overall health is good. During this physical exam, the veterinarian will listen to your cat's heart and lungs; take her temperature, pulse, and breathing rate; weigh her; check the eyes, ears, and skin for infection or parasites; look inside the mouth to make sure there's no tartar buildup on teeth or other dental problems; and palpate (feel) her body to make sure the organs don't seem enlarged and that there are no suspicious lumps or bumps that could indicate infections or tumors. The annual exam is also a good time to take in a fecal sample to make sure your cat doesn't have any intestinal parasites—unlikely if she's an indoor cat. Besides this annual exam, your cat should go to the veterinarian any time she has a serious injury or illness. Minor bouts of vomiting or diarrhea usually aren't a problem, but a visit to the veterinarian is warranted if vomiting or diarrhea is frequent or lasts for more than forty-eight hours, if the cat's behavior is unusual—say, lack of appetite for more than a day—or if the cat suffers a serious injury that causes lameness or that you can't treat with your feline first-aid kit. Following are some of the signs or events that indicate a trip to the veterinarian is warranted:

- Pain. Cats are subtle creatures, and they're relatively inactive, so it can be difficult to tell when they're in pain. Watch for changes such as eating less, failing to greet you at the door when that's a normal behavior, flinching during grooming, or crying out when picked up. These are significant changes in behavior that can indicate pain. Refusing petting, no longer jumping up to high places, stiffness, decreased mobility, and limping are other signs that a cat may be in pain.
- Pale or discolored gums. A cat's gums are normally a healthy pink color. If you press on the gum of a healthy cat, it loses color and then rapidly regains it. If your cat's gums are pale or are slow to refill with color, she may be anemic. Bluish-gray gums indicate shock or dehydration. In either case, take your cat to the veterinarian.
- Runny nose or sneezing. Cats are prone to serious respiratory disease. If your cat has a runny nose for several hours or persistent sneezing, she may be showing the first signs of viral respiratory disease. Get her to the veterinarian as soon as possible.
- Lack of appetite. A cat that wants to eat but doesn't, or that picks up food and then drops it, may have a dental problem or other mouth disease. Other signs of mouth disease are drooling and bad breath.
- Lethargy. This might be difficult to recognize in an adult cat, but in a kitten it's obvious. Any time a normally active and

high-spirited kitten droops for more than twenty-four hours, it's time to see a veterinarian.

- Trauma. Being hit by a car, electrical shock, a bite from a dog or other animal, exposure to excessive heat or cold, and similar serious events call for an immediate visit to the veterinary clinic.

CHAPTER 8

Feeding Your
New Cat

WE ALL LEARN in grade school that you are what you eat. That old chestnut holds true for cats as well. Good nutrition plays a major role in your cat's good health. The right diet can make a dramatic difference in a cat's appearance, activity level, and resistance to diseases. Many cat owners, including myself, have seen a tangible change in their cats' health after switching to higher-quality foods.

Good nutrition, then, is the foundation of a long and healthy life. Food contains nutrients that enable the body to form strong bones and muscles, supple skin, and a lush coat, as well as a powerful immune system to fight off diseases.

What do cats need from their diets? Like us, they need a diet that provides proteins, fats, carbohydrates, vitamins, minerals, and water. These nutrients work in combination to keep the body functioning at peak efficiency. When the level of nutrients is out of whack—due to a poor diet, for instance—the body functions less efficiently. Hair becomes dull or falls out, teeth loosen, eyes lose their shine, and the skin loses elasticity. It's easy to tell at a glance when your cat isn't eating correctly. Here's what you need to know about nutrients:

- Protein is the most important nutrient cats need. Descended from meat-eating desert animals, cats are obligate carnivores, meaning they must have meat-based protein in their diets. That's because cats are unable to synthesize certain amino acids, such as taurine, which are found only in meat. Amino acids are protein's building blocks, necessary for creating enzymes, hormones, and antibodies. Proteins are the body's means of transforming food into energy, and they add flavor to a diet, very important to a cat. Cats require more protein than either dogs or humans, so never assume that your cat can get by on the dog's food. Meat is the best source of protein for a cat.
- Fats are also essential for cats. They keep the skin and coat healthy, provide energy, and add flavor. Fat pads the vital organs, protecting them from injury, and helps insulate the body. Cats require more and different fatty acids than dogs, another reason why dog food is never an adequate diet for a cat. Typical sources of fat in cat food are animal fats and vegetable oils.
- For people and dogs, carbohydrates (sugars and starches) provide an easy and efficient source of energy, but for cats they're not very digestible. The best diet for a cat is one that's high in protein and fat, with some carbohydrates to help provide extra energy. Common sources of carbohydrates are grains such as corn, rice, wheat, and oats.
- Vitamins and minerals help convert proteins, fats, and carbohydrates to energy and facilitate metabolic processes such as tissue formation and cell maintenance and growth. Proper vitamin

and mineral balance is crucial, and the use of vitamin and mineral supplements in feline diets is controversial. In most cases, providing a nutritionally complete commercial diet is enough to meet a cat's vitamin and mineral needs, but a homemade or raw diet will need supplementation.

- Water isn't commonly thought of as a nutrient, but it's essential for your cat's good health. Water makes up almost 70 percent of a cat's body and plays a vital role in cell and organ function. Cats can go for weeks without food, but without water they can die in a few days. Your cat should have an ample supply of fresh water daily. The average cat needs an ounce of water per pound of body weight daily. For a ten-pound cat, that's about one and a quarter cups, which can be obtained by drinking and from eating canned food (which is about 70 percent water).

Now that you know a little bit about nutrients, the next step is to choose an appropriate diet. That can be hard to do, with all the choices you'll see on the grocery store or pet supply store shelves. Cat food manufacturers have come up with a number of formulas to meet the needs of cats in all life stages. They also describe their foods with terms that sound good—premium, super premium, quality, natural—but have no legal or scientific definition. You also need to decide whether to feed your cat a dry or canned commercial diet or if you want to go the homemade or raw route, a choice that is becoming increasingly common among cat owners.

Because each cat is an individual with unique needs, there is no right or wrong answer to some of these questions. Just as not every food is tasty or agreeable to us, not every diet is best for all cats. Choosing the right food is a matter of experimenting to find a high-quality diet that suits your individual cat's nutritional needs.

Factors to consider when deciding how and what to feed your cat include what the label tells you, palatability (does your cat like the taste?), price, availability, and—if you're considering a homemade diet—the amount of time you have to spend preparing food. Ask your veterinarian and—if applicable—the breeder for advice, and don't be afraid to try different foods until you find the one you and your cat like best. The following questions and answers can help you understand what to look for in a food, how to read a label, and how to feed your cat appropriately.

LABEL LAW

What kind of information can I expect to find on a cat food label?

By law, a cat food label must contain the following information:

- Product name
- Net weight
- Name and address of the manufacturer
- The ingredients, listed in descending order by weight
- Guaranteed analysis
- The words "cat food"
- A statement of nutritional adequacy
- A statement of the methods used to substantiate nutritional adequacy
- Feeding directions

Federal and state regulations also call for very specific descriptions of ingredients and quantities in pet foods. It takes a little reading between the lines, but you can get a good idea of a cat food's quality simply by taking a good, hard look at the label.

FELINE FEAST

CAT FOOD

Net Wt 2.1 OZ (59.5 g)

INGREDIENTS: Deboned Chicken, Chicken Meal, Chicken Liver, Ground Brown Rice, Ground Whole Oats, Canola Oil (Preserved with Mixed Tocopherols & Rosemary), Cranberries, Blueberries, Flax Seed, Eggs, Peas, Taurine, Garlic, Alfalfa Leaf, Spirulina, Norwegian Kelp, Whole Apples, Zucchini, Sweet Potatoes, Yucca Schidigera, Chondroitin Sulfate, Glucosamine, Pro-Biotics (Lactobacillus Plantarum, Enterococcus Faecium, Lactobacillus Casei, Lactobacillus Acidophilus), Pre-Biotics (Mannanoligosaccharides), Beta-Carotene, Choline Chloride, Calcium Carbonate, Zinc Proteinate (a Chelated Source of Zinc), Vitamin E Supplement, Zinc Oxide, Ferrous Sulfate, Iron Proteinate (a Chelated Source of Iron), Manganese Proteinate (a Chelated Source of Manganese), Calcium Pantothenate, Niacin Supplement, Sodium Selenite, Vitamin A Acetate, Folic Acid, Cobalt Proteinate (a Chelated Source of Cobalt), Copper Sulfate, Cobalt Carbonate, Riboflavin Supplement (Vitamin B-2), Copper Proteinate (a Chelated Source of Copper), Thiamine Mononitrate (Vitamin B-1), Vitamin D-3 Supplement, Calcium Iodate, Pyridoxine Hydrochloride, Menadione Sodium Bisulfite Complex (Source of Vitamin K Activity).

GUARANTEED ANALYSIS:	
CRUDE PROTEIN (MIN)	31.0%
CRUDE FAT (MIN)	10.0%
CRUDE FIBER (MAX)	4.5%
MOISTURE (MAX)	10.0%
LINOLEIC ACID (MIN)	0.5%
ARACHIDONIC ACID (MIN)	0.02%
CALCIUM (MIN)	1.2%
PHOSPHORUS (MIN)	1.0%
POTASSIUM (MIN)	0.6%
SODIUM (MIN)	0.2%
CHLORIDE (MIN)	0.3%
CHOLINE (MIN)	2,400 MG/KG
TAURINE (MIN)	0.1%

NUTRITIONAL STATEMENT:
ANIMAL FEEDING TESTS USING AAFCO PROCEDURES SUBSTANTIATE THAT FELINE FEAST PROVIDES COMPLETE AND BALANCED NUTRITION FOR MAINTENANCE OF THE ADULT CAT.

FEEDING INSTRUCTIONS:
Feed one can daily per 8 pounds of body weight. Adjust to maintain ideal body weight.

To help ensure good health, feed your cat the highest quality food you can afford.

WHAT'S IN A NAME

What can the product name tell me? That doesn't seem very helpful.

Believe it or not, the product name is a good place to start. The U.S. Food and Drug Administration's (FDA) Center for Veterinary Medicine sets strict guidelines on what a food can be called. Here's what to look for.

If a food is called Cat's Meow Tuna for Cats, the food must contain 95 percent tuna, not counting the water used for processing. Taking the water into account, the food would still be required to contain at least 70 percent tuna. (By the way, tuna is fine as an occasional treat for cats, but it's unhealthy as a sole diet.) Let's say the name includes a combination of ingredients, such as Cat's Meow Tuna and Salmon for Cats. Then tuna and salmon must make up 95 percent of the total weight excluding water, and the food must contain more tuna than salmon.

There's more. Perhaps you're looking at Cat's Meow Chicken Dinner for Cats. Whether the food is canned or dry, chicken must make up at least 25 percent of the product, exclusive of water. In other words, any time a food contains at least 25 percent of a named ingredient—chicken, in this case—but less than 95 percent, it must include a qualifying description such as dinner, platter, entrée, nuggets, stew, or formula. When you look at the label for this food, the chicken might be third or fourth on the ingredient list, instead of first, where it belongs. What if Cat's Meow makes a Chicken and Fish Dinner? Together, the two named ingredients must total 25 percent of the product, with at least 3 percent fish. There will always be more of the ingredient that's listed first. Sometimes manufacturers like to highlight a minor ingredient such as cheese or bacon. They can do this if the food contains at least 3 percent of the highlighted ingredient. If you see Cat's Meow Fish Dinner for Cats "with cheese," you know that it contains at least 3 percent cheese. If it reads "with cheese and bacon," it must contain at least 3 percent of each ingredient.

What if you see a food called Cat's Meow Salmon Flavor Cat Food? A food with the word "flavor" in the name isn't required to have a specific percentage of the given flavor, but it must be detectable. Expect to see salmon meal, salmon by-products, or salmon digests listed on the label to provide flavor. With the exception of artificial smoke or bacon flavors, which are often added to treats, pet foods rarely contain artificial flavors.

INGREDIENT INFORMATION

What else should I look for on the label?

Pay attention to the way ingredients are listed on the side of the bag or can. They must be listed in order by weight. For instance, if the first ingredient is chicken meal, followed by brown rice, you can assume that the primary source of protein is animal based, as it should be for a cat. The downside is that you can't determine the quality of a cat food's ingredients based on the ingredient list, only whether they're primarily of animal or plant origin. Always choose a food that has more meat-based protein than grain-based protein.

CAT-TESTED AND APPROVED?

I've heard that I should only buy foods that use AAFCO feeding trials to determine whether they meet a cat's nutritional needs. What's AAFCO, and are feeding trials really important?

The American Association of Feed Control Officials sets nutrient profiles for cats in all life stages: growth, adult maintenance, and pregnancy and lactation, for instance. A food must contain the correct levels of all the nutrients a cat needs before it can be labeled "complete and balanced." AAFCO requires pet food manufacturers to prove their claims through feeding trials or chemical analysis. A product that has been tested with feeding trials will carry a statement that reads "Animal feeding tests using AAFCO procedures substantiate that (name of product) provides complete and balanced nutrition." Most reputable commercial manufacturers perform feeding trials of their foods.

AAFCO feeding trials are considered the best way to determine whether a food meets a cat's nutritional needs, and there's some validity to that statement. Feeding trials provide tangible evidence that a cat is able to digest and absorb the nutrients. But Jean Hofve, DVM, points out some potential drawbacks as well. "When you look at the actual AAFCO protocols for an adult maintenance diet, a manufacturer must feed exclusively the test food to only six animals for six months," she says. "Foods intended for growth and reproduction must be tested for only 10 weeks." In both cases, that's not a very big test population nor a very long test period. "It's easy to see how a poor-quality diet could be fed for only six months without seeing adverse health effects, and legitimately be labeled as meeting AAFCO standards," Dr. Hofve says.

This is when you need to take into consideration the manufacturer's reputation. "Most of the large, reputable pet food producers, such as Iams, Hills, Waltham, and Purina, maintain large colonies of cats and dogs and test their foods on hundreds of animals over years or even multiple generations," Dr. Hofve says. "Other manufacturers rely on facilities that keep animals for this purpose to do the studies for them." If you're concerned, contact the company—remember, their address must be included on the label—and ask for details on how they test their foods. Most companies have a toll-free number you can call to get information about their foods.

Finally, Dr. Hofve says, keep in mind that the standards set only minimums and maximums, not optimums. "Commercial foods are designed to be adequate for the average animals, but may not be suitable for an individual animal's variable needs," she says. If your cat isn't thriving on a particular food, no matter how good it is, he may need a different diet.

NUTRITIONAL ADEQUACY

What's the difference between foods for kittens and adult cats?

Kittens need high levels of nutrients to fuel their rapid growth. Adult cats with normal activity levels don't need the extra calories or nutrients found in kitten foods. If you look at the nutritional adequacy statement on the food you're considering, it will say which life stage the food is meant for, such as "for maintenance" or "for growth." According to the Food and Drug Administration's Center for Veterinary Medicine (CVM), a maintenance diet isn't sufficient for a growing kitten, but an "all life stages" food can be used for maintenance. These higher levels of nutrients aren't harmful to a healthy adult cat, but they aren't really necessary. You may see a label that states "this product is intended for intermittent or supplemental feeding." That means that it's not complete and balanced and should not be fed as a sole diet.

PRICEY PET FOODS

The "super premium" and "natural" foods sold in pet supply stores are so much more expensive than what I find in the grocery store. Are they really better for my cat?

The first thing to know is that foods labeled with such terms as "premium," "super premium," or "gourmet" are not required to contain any different or higher-quality ingredients than any other complete and balanced products, according to the CVM. Nor does the term "natural" have an official definition. It's usually used in reference to foods that don't contain artificial flavors, colors, or preservatives. It's also important to note that "natural" is not the same as "organic." The word organic refers to the conditions under which plants were grown or animals raised. At this time, there are no official rules governing the labeling of organic foods for cats.

That said, premium foods do tend to have higher-quality ingredients than the brands you might find at the grocery store. Generally, the difference between premium and nonpremium foods is density per volume. In other words, a tablespoon of a premium food is likely to have more nutrients that are digested and absorbed than a tablespoon of nonpremium food. What that means is that the higher cost of a premium food is made up in savings of amount served and later eliminated by the cat. Paradoxically, it can cost less to feed a high-quality food, because your cat is eating less of it but getting a higher percentage of nutrients.

Nonetheless, plenty of veterinarians, breeders, and cat owners say that national-brand foods sold in grocery stores are just as high in nutrition as pricier premium brands. The corporations that make national-brand cat food—whether it's premium or a grocery store brand—all spend big bucks on nutritional studies and feeding trials. The price differences you see are usually based on types and amounts of ingredients. For instance, a premium food might contain organic lamb or wild salmon or grain that's grown without the use of pesticides. It might contain more animal protein than grain protein or be free of by-products, dyes, or synthetic preservatives.

The other advantage of premium foods is that they are made according to fixed formulas, meaning that the ingredients don't change from batch to batch. Some less expensive foods may have varying ingredients depending on what grain, for instance, is least expensive at the time the company is buying.

Again, don't be afraid to call the company's toll-free hotline and ask exactly what they mean by the terms "organic" or "natural" or "human-grade." When you choose a food, decide what's important to you, and then see how your cat does on it. That's the real test of a food's quality.

BRAND X

Is it okay to feed my cat a generic food?

Without exception that I'm aware of, feline nutrition experts advise against feeding generic, or no-name, foods. Their nutritional adequacy is rarely substantiated by feeding trials, and they generally contain low-quality ingredients that vary from batch to batch depending on what's cheapest and most available. It's more economical in the long run to feed your cat a high-quality food. You'll see the savings in lower veterinary bills.

DRY VERSUS CANNED

Is dry food or canned food better for my cat?

That depends on who you talk to. Generally speaking, any dry or canned food that is complete and balanced will meet your cat's nutritional needs. Arguments have been made over the years that dry food is better for dental health (this has been disproved) or that canned food is more appetizing to cats. The choice you make depends on your cat's dietary needs and preferences, as well as your preferences and budget. What's most important is whether a particular food meets your cat's nutritional needs.

Canned foods contain either blends of ingredients—muscle meats or poultry, grains, vitamins, and minerals—or one or two types of muscle meats or animal by-products with enough supplemental vitamins and minerals to ensure that the food is nutritionally complete. Depending on the ingredients used, canned foods can vary widely in nutrient content, digestibility, and availability of nutrients. They're prepared by cooking and blending all of the ingredients, canning and cooking the mixture, and pressure sterilizing the sealed can.

Cats love canned food. It meets their "smells good, tastes good" criteria. That's because canned food has a high fat content and is calorically dense. Canned food has a long shelf life, although it must be refrigerated after it's opened. It's easier to eat for older cats that have difficulty chewing. And for you, it's easy enough to open a can and dump the contents into your cat's dish. And some veterinarians believe that the water in canned food helps reduce the workload on the kidneys and keep the urine dilute.

Canned food does have disadvantages. It's expensive. Its water content is high—as much as 78 percent—so you're not getting a lot of meat for your money. You can't leave it out for long periods, and leftovers must be refrigerated.

Dry food is probably the most common type of cat food purchased. Kibble contains grains, meat, poultry or fish, some milk products, and vitamin and mineral supplements. It's made by combining all the ingredients, extruding them into the desired shapes or sizes, and baking it. Once the food has cooled, the kibble is sprayed with fat or some other substance to make it taste good.

The big advantage to dry food is cost. It's much less expensive than canned food. This is something to consider when you have one or more cats to feed. Dry food has a long shelf life and can be left out without risk of going bad. On the downside, dry food generally contains less fat and more carbohydrates than canned food. Cats don't metabolize carbohydrates as well as they do meat-based proteins, and a high-carb diet can contribute to obesity.

If given a choice, most cats prefer canned food (tastes great!), while most owners prefer dry food (less expensive!). You can always compromise by mixing dry and canned foods.

DRY FOOD DENTAL BENEFITS

Is dry food better for my cat's teeth?

Dry food has a reputation for helping to prevent the buildup of plaque and tartar on teeth. Dry foods and biscuits can help crack off tartar (the hardened form of plaque), but they don't affect the gumline area. The exception to this is veterinary foods that are designed to reduce levels of plaque and tartar, so the mouth is less conducive to the growth of harmful bacteria.

The bottom line? Regular dry food helps a little in scraping tartar off teeth, but it's not a substitute for brushing. If your cat is prone to tartar buildup, your veterinarian may recommend a dental diet. If you use one of these foods, be sure it's complete and balanced for your cat's life stage.

OTHER TYPES OF FOODS

My pet supply store has a frozen-food section now. Are there any advantages to a frozen diet?

Frozen cat foods are made with fresh meat, vegetables, and fruit, and contain no artificial preservatives. After being mixed and formed into loaves, rolls, patties, or cubes, the food is flash frozen to preserve freshness. Frozen nuggets are as easy to feed as dry food (as long as you remember to defrost them in advance), and loaves or rolls are easy to slice after defrosting. Consider a commercial frozen food if you like the idea of fresh ingredients but don't have time to cook for the cat yourself.

The down side is that frozen cat food is usually available only in limited distribution. Not all pet stores carry it, and you may have to have it delivered by mail or by a local distributor. It must be kept frozen until you're ready to use it, and any unused portion must be refrigerated. If you're traveling with a cat, it's difficult to take the food along unless you have some means of refrigeration or of finding it in pet stores along the way. Some frozen foods also come in freeze-dried form and can be reconstituted with hot water. Some cats will eat this, while others turn up their noses.

FEEDING GUIDELINES

How much should I feed my cat?

Just as with palatability or sensitivity to a particular ingredient, cats are individuals when it comes to portion size. The feeding directions on the package are guidelines only. They give you a starting point for the amount your cat should be eating, and you can adjust the amount up or down as needed.

Let your cat's condition be your guide. If he's putting on weight, cut back a little on the food. If he looks thin, add some more. Your veterinarian or the breeder can also help you determine the right amount.

TWO SQUARES A DAY

How often should I feed my cat?

For many years, cat experts recommended free-feeding cats; that is, leaving food out for them all the time. Cats have a reputation as nibblers, and they've been known to eat up to sixteen small meals per day. Based on the latest epidemiological studies, though, free-feeding cats is no longer recommended, for a couple of reasons. For one, cats that have constant access to a highly palatable, high-fat diet tend to eat too much and get fat. For another, cats that always have food available can become bored or finicky, leading to behavior problems.

The latest advice is to feed a cat a specified amount twice a day, taking the food up after an hour. That's not all. Many cat behaviorists now recommend that owners (especially those who are gone during the day) place a cat's morning meal—dry food, of course—inside a play and treat ball so that the cat has to make an effort to get his food. This serves two purposes: it keeps the cat entertained during the day by letting him practice his "hunting" techniques, and it allows him to nibble as he pleases, while still limiting the amount of food he has available. The extra activity also helps prevent obesity, which is the number one nutritional disorder in cats.

HOMEMADE DIETS

My cousin feeds her cats a homemade raw diet. Is this really healthy?

Cat owners have joined the trend toward healthy eating, with more and more of them showing an interest in preparing a homemade or raw diet for their animals. The attraction of this type of diet is that you can control the quality of the ingredients. You may also want to use a homemade diet if your cat has food allergies, is sensitive to artificial dyes or preservatives, or has a particular health problem that can be helped by a special diet.

Proponents of raw diets argue that they are more natural and provide better nutrition. Raw foods retain enzymes and other healthful substances that cooking destroys. People who use raw diets say their cats have better health, a beautiful coat, few or no skin problems, and great teeth. Factors to consider before deciding on a homemade or raw diet include nutritional completeness, time, and expense.

One of the concerns about homemade diets is that they may lack certain vitamins and minerals or contain an improper balance of protein, fats, and carbohydrates. Simply feeding human-grade products doesn't make a diet complete and balanced. If ingredients aren't provided in proper proportions, the diet may be inadequate. It's possible to design a nutritionally complete homemade diet for cats, but it's important to use appropriate recipes from valid sources. Look for a book by a veterinary nutritionist or a layperson trained in nutrition.

You can find many excellent books, articles, and Web sites with detailed guidelines on ingredients, proportions, and preparation of homemade cat foods. Don't just throw some meat and rice together and think that's a good diet for your cat, because it's not.

If you want to feed your cat a homemade diet for the health benefits, you'll want to use only the best and freshest ingredients, not leftovers or the butcher's scraps. High-quality ingredients are expensive. This is especially true if you want to stick to organic meats and vegetables, which are free of potentially harmful hormones, antibiotics, pesticides, and herbicides. It's a good idea to rotate the meats, vegetables, and fruits you use so that your cat receives a variety of nutrients and stays interested in her meals. Cats that eat only one type of food for extended periods are prone to diet-induced diseases such as skin problems and vitamin and mineral deficiencies. If you use a homemade raw diet, it's a good idea to have your cat's blood tested periodically to make sure she's not suffering from any vitamin or mineral deficiencies.

Commercial cat foods come ready to go in bags or cans. They're easy to measure out and feed. For a homemade diet, ingredients must be purchased, measured, mixed, and cooked (unless you're feeding your cat a raw diet) on a frequent basis. If you enjoy cooking and have plenty of time to spend in the kitchen, this isn't a drawback.

HEALTH CONCERNS

Is raw food safe?

One of the greatest concerns people have about feeding their cats raw food is the fear of bacterial infection, either in themselves or their cats. Cat owners who neglect safe handling practices are undoubtedly more at risk of infection from E. coli and salmonella, as well as staphylococcus, listeria, and toxoplasmosis, especially if they have compromised immune systems. Almost all foods purchased from the grocery store have bacteria present on them. However, it's important to remember that many of these bacteria live naturally in the intestinal tract of humans and cats. Only specific strains of specific bacteria have the potential to cause disease and then only when their numbers reach high levels. If pathogenic (disease-causing) bacteria are present when food is purchased and safe handling procedures aren't followed, the organisms may proliferate to a point where their numbers can cause disease in humans. They usually aren't a problem if proper precautions are taken. Here are some safe handling practices to follow if you're preparing raw food for your cat:

- Defrost meat in the refrigerator instead of on the kitchen counter.
- Wash your hands before and after touching raw meat.
- Use hot, soapy water to clean and disinfect dishes, utensils, cutting boards, grinders, and other equipment used to prepare meals.
- Refrigerate or freeze raw food if you don't plan to feed it immediately.

COMMERCIAL NATURAL CAT FOOD

I can barely get dinner on the table for my family, let alone for the cat, but I'm not satisfied with the products available at the grocery store. What can I do?

You may want to consider purchasing a natural or raw-diet food from a pet supply store or through mail order. Many companies produce organic or raw-diet food for cats that are preservative-free and contain high-quality ingredients.

SWITCHING DIETS

What's the best way to introduce a new food to my cat?

Cats tend to have sensitive digestive systems, so switching them to a new food is best done slowly to prevent vomiting or diarrhea. Add a new food gradually, mixing increasing amounts of it with the previous food over a period of five to ten days, until the cat is eating only the new food.

FINICKY FELINE

My cat will eat only one flavor and brand of cat food, but I'd like to add some variety to his diet as well as improve the quality of the food he's getting. How can I persuade him to try something new?

Cats have a reputation for being finicky, and sometimes it's deserved. Kitties are conservatives at heart, and they're not especially fond of change. It can help to feed your cat twice a day (if you're not already doing so), leaving the food down for no more than an hour. Many finicky cats turn up their nose at something different, simply because they're not hungry. Cats are meant to eat about once a day, and eating more often kills their appetite. If you limit the amount of time food is left out for them, they'll be more interested in eating what you give them at the established mealtime, even if it isn't their favorite.

Never "starve" your cat, thinking that she'll eat if she gets hungry enough. This can cause serious health problems. Instead, try feeding the mix of old and new foods in the morning, withholding the cat's desired food until the evening mealtime. Your cat may be willing to at least nibble on the food provided at breakfast, if that's all there is. It's also a good idea to experiment with different meats or flavors when you're introducing a new food. You may hit on one that your cat likes just as much as the old food.

To avoid creating food addictions in cats, rotate different meats and flavors into the diet on a regular basis. If your cat is accustomed to a changing diet from the start, he'll be less likely to become finicky. Adaptability could save your cat's life if he ever becomes ill and needs to follow a special diet. A varied diet can also help prevent nutritional deficiencies that might develop when a cat eats only one type of food (tuna, for instance).

TABLE SCRAPS

My cat loves to lick my plate after I'm done eating. Is it okay to let him do that?

Letting your cat lick a little egg yolk off your plate or giving him a small bite of meat that's not highly seasoned or sauced is okay, but table scraps in large amounts are unhealthy treats.

TREAT TIME

My cat loves the treats "Grandma" buys her from the grocery store. Are these a healthy part of her diet?

Everyone loves a treat now and then, including cats. Treats are great for rewarding your cat during training or simply giving her something special because you love her. As long as they don't exceed 5 to 10 percent of your cat's daily calorie intake, it's fine to give her treats. Just be sure to avoid chocolate, which is toxic to cats, and fatty meats, which can cause an upset stomach or, more seriously, an inflammation of the pancreas.

MILK LOVER

My cat Moscow likes to drink the leftover milk from my cereal bowl, but I heard that cats are lactose-intolerant. Should I stop letting Moscow do this?

You'd be surprised at the number of cat owners who share their morning cereal with their cats. It's true that some adult cats can't tolerate milk sugar (lactose). They aren't able to digest it and subsequently develop diarrhea. If Moscow doesn't suffer this side effect, it's all right to continue letting her have small amounts of milk.

WEIRD ABOUT WATER

My cat likes to drink from dripping faucets. He even learned to push the handle to turn it on himself. What's up with that?

Believe it or not, lots of cats like to drink running water. It might be that they're attracted by the movement of the water as it falls into the sink, or maybe they just have some ancestral memory of drinking from a refreshing stream. Whatever the case, your cat isn't alone. Many cats demand that a faucet be left dripping for them at all times or, like your cat, they learn to turn the water on for themselves. You can even purchase a drinking fountain for your cat so he'll always have a fresh supply of running water. The veterinarian who designed the Drinkwell Pet Fountain says it encourages cats to drink and discourages them from jumping on counters in search of dripping faucets. My cats were afraid of it, but for your cat it might be just the ticket.

WEIRD ABOUT WATER, TAKE TWO

My cat will only drink out of the dogs' metal water dish, even though she has one just like it in the kitchen. She refuses to use anything else. Why is she so fussy?

What can I say? Cats can be strange, especially when it comes to their drinking habits. Some like to drink out of the toilet, some from a running faucet (see above), and some from a particular type of dish or a dish in a certain spot. Others dip a paw into water and then lick the drops off. Some cats flip out if you add ice cubes to their water dish or make some other seemingly inconsequential change. These drinking preferences are set at an early age, and it's next to impossible to change them. Be glad that your cat has a favorite drinking spot, and tell the dogs to share.

CALORIE COUNT

How many calories per day does a cat need?

That depends on her age and activity level. A ten-week-old kitten needs about 113 calories per pound of body weight. By the time she's five months old, her caloric needs have dropped by almost half, to 59 calories per pound of body weight. An adult cat needs 32 to 36 calories per pound of body weight, depending on how active she is. For a ten-pound cat, that would be 320 to 360 calories per day. Pregnant cats or those that are nursing kittens need extra calories.

THE RIGHT FOOD

How can I tell if the food I've chosen is right for my cat?

That's easy. If you're not sure whether a food is doing your cat good, just take a look at him and let his condition be your guide. If his coat looks great, his energy level is high, his eyes are clear, and the stools you clean out of the litter box are small and firm, you can be reasonably sure that the food you're giving is doing its job.

FAT CAT DIET PLAN

Obesity—defined as weighing 15 percent or more over the recommended body weight—is the number one nutritional problem in cats. Fat cats are predisposed to such health problems as liver failure, urinary tract problems, bladder stones, diabetes, and respiratory and cardiac disorders. They're more likely to become lame from arthritis because of the extra weight they carry or to develop nonallergic skin conditions because they're not able to groom themselves properly. (It's hard to lick your tail when your stomach keeps getting in the way!) If your veterinarian has told you that your cat is too fat and needs to lose weight, the following diet and exercise program can help him regain a sleek physique.

To help your cat lose weight, start by decreasing the amount of food he gets. Do this gradually, until he's eating 20 to 30 percent less than what he was originally getting. An easy way to do this is to replace the measuring cup you've been using to scoop out the food with one of a smaller size.

Cut way back on any treats or table scraps, and be sure the whole family knows not to sneak him food. If you want to give him treats, stick with healthful snacks, such as fruits and vegetables. Many cats love cantaloupe or bits of carrots and green beans.

At the same time, gradually increase his activity level. Tailor the workout to your cat's physical condition. If he's middle-aged or old, overweight, inactive, and breathes heavily at the slightest exertion, get your veterinarian's okay before starting an exercise plan, and go slowly. Start with a gentle two-minute workout and gradually increase the time and amount of exertion as his condition improves. Ways to get your cat moving include putting his dry food inside a play and treat ball (a paper towel tube works, too) so he has to put forth some effort to get it, dangling a large feather or fishing-pole toy for him to bat at, beaming a flashlight or laser pen for him to chase, and encouraging him to scratch on and climb up his scratching post.

CHAPTER 9

Grooming Your New Cat

GROOMING IS ONE of the first lines of defense when it comes to keeping a cat healthy. Regular grooming familiarizes you with your cat's body so you come to know what's normal and what's not. Depending on your cat's condition, you'll notice reactions of pleasure or discomfort. The grooming session is a good time to examine your cat for lumps, parasites, and sores. Combing and brushing also strengthen the bond between you and your cat.

In addition to the emotional benefits of the human-feline bond, grooming is psychologically important to cats. They like to be clean and will spend hours licking their coats into shape. An unkempt cat is usually an unhealthy, unhappy cat. If your cat has no desire to groom herself, she may not be feeling well.

Naturally, grooming also has physical benefits. The skin is the body's largest organ, a protective covering that wraps the body and acts as a shield and sensor. The skin guards against invasion by bacteria and helps the body retain moisture, preventing dehydration. Beneath the skin lie the sebaceous glands. They secrete a substance called sebum, which gives hair an oily, protective coating and keeps it soft and supple, flexible enough to bend without breaking. Frequent brushing helps keep these oils distributed and the cat's coat shiny. Regular brushing also helps to prevent hairballs from forming and mats from developing in cats with long fur. Depending on your cat's coat type, grooming should take place daily or weekly. Cats with coats that mat easily, such as Persians, usually need daily brushing and combing. Shorthaired cats can get by with combing or brushing just once a week. Other aspects of grooming include trimming the nails, keeping the eyes and ears clean, and brushing the teeth. The following questions and answers will help you keep your cat looking groomed to the nines.

BRUSHING YOUR CAT

What's the best way to brush my cat?

Brushing is the foundation of good grooming. It loosens and removes dirt, dead hair, and old skin cells and distributes the skin's natural oils through the coat. To brush a shorthaired cat, use a wire slicker brush, grooming mitt, or rubber curry brush. You can also use a fine- or medium-toothed comb. Start at the cat's head and work your way over the body to the tail. Don't skip the stomach area, even if your cat resists lying on her side or back. Be sure to brush all the way down to the skin, not just over the surface of the coat. Always brush in the same direction the coat lies. When you're finished, give your cat's coat a glossy shine by polishing it with a chamois cloth or rubbing your hands over the coat with long, smooth strokes.

For a longhaired cat, use a wide-toothed metal comb. As described above, start at the head and work your way back. Then go over the coat in the same way with a pin brush, which has stiff nylon or metal bristles set wide apart. This helps remove loose hair. Be sure you don't miss the areas behind the ears and at the juncture where the legs join the body. These are prime places for mats to form. If your longhaired cat has a tangle, gently try to work it out using a tangle remover spray and a wide-toothed comb. If that doesn't work, you will have to cut it away. Be careful not to cut into the skin.

As your hands move the brush or comb through your cat's fur, you'll learn to recognize the normal texture and condition of her coat and how her body feels.

Regularly grooming your cat is not only beneficial for his health, but is also a bonding experience for both of you.

SHEDDING LIGHT ON SHEDDING

Why do cats shed?

A cat's coat isn't just there for decoration. Fur insulates the cat's body from heat and cold and protects the skin from cuts, scrapes, and sun damage. A cat's hairs—which are complex, compact, three-dimensional structures formed by various proteins—eventually become damaged by such things as sun, dryness, and air pollutants, so the body replaces them periodically. The life cycle of hair involves growth, rest, loss, and replacement—the phenomenon we call shedding. Hairs in different parts of the body grow to genetically programmed lengths. Once they reach that length, they rest for various periods of time. Eventually, new hair pushes out the old hair, which is when it lands on your clothes, floor, and furniture.

Shedding is seasonal, with hair growth and loss taking its cue from the hours of daylight to which it's exposed. As the days grow shorter—fall into winter—the hair grows thick. As the days grow longer—spring into summer—hair begins to drop off. Outdoor cats usually shed noticeably in the spring and fall. Indoor cats, who spend long hours exposed to artificial light, tend to shed small amounts year-round. To help keep loose hair off your clothing and furniture, brush your cat daily to remove dead hair.

MORE ON SHEDDING

How much shedding is normal?

It might be better to ask what the coat looks like when a shed is normal. A cat's undercoat sheds heavily, and at times fur can look patchy. Many people take their cats to the veterinarian because they're concerned about what appears to be excessive shedding, especially when the coat looks really ratty. This usually occurs in mid-spring or mid-fall, in the case of an outdoor cat. Nonetheless, this moth-eaten look is perfectly normal. Signs of abnormal shedding are completely bald patches, which shouldn't occur with a normal shed, or symmetrical hair loss in specific areas, such as the insides of the back legs, the lower abdomen, or on the sides of the body.

FUR FRUSTRATIONS

It drives my husband crazy to find cat hair on the furniture. How can I keep things fur-free? Is there any way to keep my cat from shedding?

To keep hair from flying all over your house while you brush your cat, stage your grooming session outdoors if possible. Your cat will probably like being brushed while lying on a sunny patio. If grooming outdoors isn't feasible or safe, try setting up a grooming station in the garage or laundry (on top of the washer or dryer can be a good spot), or brush your cat while she's sitting on a sheet or large towel. When you're done, you can just throw it in the washing machine. This will help keep hair from getting in your carpet, on your furniture, or lodging in corners.

As far as keeping your cat from shedding, well, shedding is a natural process that's not likely to go away. There are some things you can try to help reduce shedding, however. One trick is to wipe your cat down periodically with a damp washcloth to lift off loose fur. Or look for specially treated wipes, made to attract and remove hair, available in pet supply stores.

It's often suggested that dietary supplementation with brewers yeast can reduce shedding. This hasn't been proven scientifically, but it can't hurt to give it a try.

HAIRBALL HOTLINE

My cat is always throwing up hairballs. Is there any way to prevent them?

One of the easiest ways to prevent hairballs is to brush your cat daily. A couple of minutes removing loose hair with the brush means that your cat won't ingest the hair when she grooms herself. Loose hair forms a ball in the stomach, and then gets vomited up, usually in dramatic and noisy fashion in the middle of a dinner party. You can also ask your veterinarian to recommend a petroleum-based hairball remedy that you can administer on a daily basis. You can let your cat lick it off your finger or apply it to her paws for her to lick off. Some treats are formulated to contain mineral oil, which helps break up hair balls.

SHAVE SOLUTION

I can't keep up with the mats that form in my Persian's coat. Can I just shave her?

If you don't mind not having a cat with the Persian look, shaving can be a good solution. Take the cat to a professional groomer and ask for a lion clip. The groomer will shave the body, leaving a pom-pom at the tip of the tail and on the feet. If you decide to do this, don't forget to protect your cat's now bare skin from extremes of heat and cold.

SUDDENLY SHEDDING

My cat sheds like crazy whenever I take her to the veterinarian. What causes this?

Fright or stress can cause sudden hair shedding. Many people notice this phenomenon when they take their cats to the veterinarian or during any other stressful experience. This occurrence is believed to be a loss of telogen hairs—those in the resting stage of the hair growth cycle—caused when fright or stress activate the arrector pili muscles. It's not harmful—except to your appearance, because most of the hair ends up on your clothes.

SPECIAL COAT CARE

*What kind of coat care does a wire-haired, curly, or hairless
cat need?*

Cats with wiry or curly coats, such as the American Wirehair, Cornish and Devon Rex, and LaPerm, have an advantage because their coats need little grooming. You can simply wipe the coat down with a chamois or soft-bristled baby brush once or twice a week. (Lots of petting helps remove dead hair too.) Using a brush—or at least the wrong kind of brush—can break off the fragile hairs or be painful to the cat. Avoid using a wire slicker brush on these breeds.

The grooming needs of the curly-coated Selkirk Rex vary according to whether the coat is short or long. In either case, however, brushing should not be frequent if you want to maintain the curly look. To help the hairs curl, use a shampoo that doesn't coat the hair but instead leaves the cat feeling silky and clean.

The Sphynx is often described as a hairless breed, but that's not entirely true; he's covered with a soft down that feels like suede to the touch. The skin becomes oily and should be wiped down frequently to prevent oily spots on furniture or clothing. Bathe the cat every week or two with a mild shampoo recommended by the breeder or your veterinarian. Whatever the breed, your cat's breeder can give you the best advice on how to groom the unusual coats of these cats.

SPF KITTY

Can cats get sunburned?

Just like people, cats can become sunburned, especially if they have light-colored fur. The nose and ears are especially at risk. Cats that get sunburned can develop squamous cell carcinoma, a type of skin cancer. Monitor your cat's sun exposure, and make sure she has a shady place to retreat to. Apply sunscreen to the nose and ears for extra protection. The Sphynx, Cornish Rex, and Devon Rex are all sensitive to the sun, so keep them indoors.

EAR CARE

Do I need to clean my cat's ears? If yes, how often should this be done?

Make ear checks a part of your weekly grooming routine. A healthy cat's ears usually don't need any cleaning, but it's a good idea to look inside them on a regular basis to check for dirt, discharge, or parasites. Some wax is okay, but you shouldn't see a large amount of wax, dirt, or debris in the ear. If you do, warm some mineral or olive oil (test it on your wrist to make sure it's not hot), put a few drops on a cotton ball, and wipe the ear out. You can use a cotton-tipped applicator to clean ear folds, but never use one to clean out the ear canal. You don't want to push gunk farther into the ear.

Give ears a good sniff. There shouldn't be any unpleasant odor. If the ears are dirty and smell bad, you should take your cat to the veterinarian to check for infection or parasites such as ear mites.

Bacterial, fungal, and yeast infections of the ears are common in cats. Signs of infection are head shaking, tilting the head to one side, scratching the ears, a bad smell coming from the ears, discharge from the ears, or a red, inflamed appearance.

Cats with ear mites shake their head and scratch their ears frequently (usually both ears are infected), and the ears exude a dark brown waxy discharge with a dry, crumbly texture. You may see white specks the size of a period—the mites—moving in the discharge. If your cat has ear mites, the ears must be thoroughly cleaned and then treated with a medication to kill the mites. Be sure to complete the entire course of medication, or the mites can reinfect the ear.

THE EYES HAVE IT

What kind of eye care does my cat need?

Healthy eyes are bright and clear, and the eyeball is white. Check the eyes regularly for redness or other signs of irritation. Wipe away discharge—sleepies—in the corners of the eyes using a cotton ball or soft washcloth moistened with warm water. Avoid rubbing the cotton ball directly over the eye, since the fibers can irritate it. Be concerned if your cat's eyes tear excessively, particularly if you have a Persian or other snub-nosed cat. Nasal-fold infections are often secondary to tearing. Other signs of eye problems include blinking, squinting, or pawing at the eye; thick, sticky, or puslike discharge; an opaque or whitish film over the eyeball; redness; swollen or crusty eyelids; and bulging or sunken eyes. Take your cat to the veterinarian if she exhibits any of these signs. Early treatment can save your cat's eyesight.

CLAW CARE

How should I trim my cat's claws, and how often should they be trimmed?

Nail care is an important part of grooming your cat. It also protects your furniture and other belongings from scratching damage. Examine nails weekly and trim them if necessary. Most cats need to have their nails trimmed every one to two weeks. You can use nail clippers made for humans (that's what I use) or purchase a clipper made for cutting cat claws.

To trim the nails, choose a time when your cat is relaxed or sleepy. As he lies on the bed or in a sunny spot, gently grasp his paw with your left hand, holding the nail clippers in your right hand. (Reverse this if you're a lefty.) Gently press upward on the pad and down behind the nail bed to extend the nail. Clip just where the nail curves. Don't clip too far past the curve or you'll hit the quick, causing the cat to bleed and yowl. If this happens, don't panic. Have a styptic pencil or styptic powder at hand so you can stop the bleeding.

Cats that become accustomed to nail trimming at an early age will put up with it without much fuss. If your cat is the exception, try holding him between your knees or wrapping him in a towel to keep him still. You may also want to ask a friend or family member to hold him while you trim the nails.

PREVENTIVE DENTAL CARE

I heard it's a good idea to brush a cat's teeth. Why is this necessary?

While cats rarely get cavities, they do get periodontal disease, an inflammation of the lining of the tooth socket. According to veterinary dentist Brook Niemiec, DVM, 70 percent of cats over two years of age have some form of periodontal disease.

Periodontal disease starts with gingivitis, the inflammation of the gingiva, or surface of the gumline. If that's not treated with proper dental cleaning and home care, the problem progresses to periodontal disease, which eventually causes the teeth to loosen and fall out. Periodontal disease doesn't just affect the teeth. Infections in the mouth can have systemic effects throughout the body. "Systemic effects of periodontal disease include kidney problems, liver problems, heart problems, lung problems," Dr. Niemiec says. "And even though the cat may not show any pain, it is affecting the animal systemically, and it's not in the cat's best interest."

DENTAL DECAY

What are the signs of periodontal disease?

Gum disease begins when food particles and saliva accumulate on the teeth, forming a soft plaque that later hardens into calculus, or tartar, which you'll recognize as a brownish buildup on teeth. The bacteria trapped in the plaque contribute to the development of gingivitis and periodontal disease. Bad breath caused by that bacteria may be the first sign you notice. One whiff of bad kitty breath, and you'll be sold on the benefits of brushing. Other signs of periodontal disease are swollen, red, or bleeding gums. Healthy gums are firm and pink. Your cat may also have periodontal disease if she's reluctant to eat, frequently drops bits of food, or doesn't want to drink cold water.

BREED PREDISPOSITION

Are some cats more prone to periodontal disease than others?

Abyssinians and Somalis and, to a certain extent, Himalayans and Siamese tend to be highly susceptible to periodontal disease, Dr. Niemiec says. "Somalis and Abys can get a certain type called refractive rapidly progressing periodontal disease. It can be so bad that their kitten teeth fall out before they're supposed to."

PEARLY WHITES

How often should I brush my cat's teeth?

Ideally, you should brush your cat's teeth every day. Plaque accumulates within twenty-four hours. If it's not removed, it hardens into calculus. Even brushing your cat's teeth three days a week will help, though, and once a week is better than nothing. If your cat refuses to have anything to do with having his teeth brushed, talk to your veterinarian about using an oral hygiene gel, which you can smear onto the surface of the gums with your fingers. These gels contain enzymes that help break down and prevent the formation of plaque. It's also a good idea to have your cat's teeth cleaned professionally every year if your cat is prone to tartar buildup.

DENTAL DOS AND DON'TS

When should I start brushing my kitten's teeth?

Start by accustoming your kitten to having your hands in her mouth. Rub the teeth gently with your finger, and praise her for letting you handle her. Don't introduce a brush until she's through teething, at six to eight months of age. Choose a gentle brush made specifically for use with cats, and use a yummy fish- or meat-flavored toothpaste. (Toothpaste made for humans can cause stomach upset.) Give her a treat when you're through.

It's really important to start brushing when a cat is young and still open to new experiences. Trying to introduce home dental hygiene to a three-year-old cat is, well, like pulling teeth.

FRACTURED FANG

My cat came in last night with a broken tooth. Now what?

Outdoor cats quite often break teeth, usually an upper canine. A broken tooth may abscess eventually, so your cat will probably need a tooth extraction or a root canal.

KITTY ORTHODONTICS

A root canal! Next you'll be telling me my cat needs braces.

Cats do occasionally get orthodontic problems, especially if they are flat-faced breeds such as Persians, which tend to have problems with their canine teeth being out of alignment. Those can be moved or-

thodontically—braces, in other words—but generally if they're causing a cat discomfort, the easiest solution is to do a pulp-capping procedure to lower the height of the tooth, Dr. Niemiec says. Grinding
the teeth down is not an option, he warns. "In a cat, especially a
young cat, you're not going to get more than a millimeter or two of
tooth structure before you've involved the root canal. I've seen a couple of cases where veterinarians have ground the teeth down and
they've become abscessed, whereas we could have taken good care of
it with a much simpler procedure."

FIGHTING FLEAS

Somehow my cat got fleas. How can I get rid of them?

Keeping a cat indoors is the easiest way to prevent flea infestation,
but if your cat goes outside or is exposed to fleas by other pets, you'll
need to use flea-control products to rid your cat of these pesky blood-
suckers. Over the years, manufacturers have worked diligently to develop products that will kill and repel fleas, and they've been quite
successful. You can purchase products that contain insect growth reg
ulators (IGRs) to prevent young fleas from developing and reproduc-
ing, and you can give your cat a flea-control pill that interferes with a
flea egg's ability to hatch. Topical (on the skin) and oral (by mouth)
medications kill adult fleas rapidly, sometimes in less than an hour.
Topical, also known as spot-on, products are applied between the
cat's shoulders or at the base of the skull and are absorbed through
the skin and distributed throughout the body. They are harmless to
the cat, and some are also effective against other parasites. These
products are available from your veterinarian and are the easiest,
most effective way to prevent flea infestations or bring them under
control.

Whatever flea product you use, make sure it's labeled for use in cats and is safe for use in kittens or old cats. Always read the label and follow the directions exactly. More is not better, so don't apply more than the directions call for. Never use products labeled for dogs or other animals. If you are using multiple products on your cat and in the environment, check with your veterinarian to make sure they're compatible.

NATURAL REMEDIES

I don't like using chemicals on my cat. Aren't there any natural flea-control remedies?

The good news is that there are lots of natural flea-control methods, such as borate powder; nematodes; brewers yeast or garlic tablets; and herbal collars, powders, and shampoos. The bad news is that their effectiveness hasn't been proven scientifically. Some people say they work great, while others don't have any luck with them.

Borate powder is one natural remedy that is pretty effective. It's found in certain powder-based carpet formulas and kills adult fleas, eggs, and larvae by removing the moisture from their bodies.

A good outdoor treatment to try is the use of nematodes, tiny organisms that eat flea larvae. You can buy nematodes at plant nurseries or through garden supply catalogs. A batch of nematodes should last about a month.

What about garlic? The theory is that cats that eat garlic don't taste good to fleas. No controlled, scientific studies have proven garlic's efficacy in flea control, but small amounts of it can't hurt and may even help, given the many anecdotal claims of its effectiveness. Holistic veterinarians advise, however, that you shouldn't rely totally on garlic as a flea-control method. And because of garlic's anticlotting properties, you should avoid giving it to cats with anemia or cats that are scheduled for surgery.

How much garlic is okay? For the average ten-pound cat, half a small clove a day is plenty. Fresh garlic is reputed to be more effective than powdered garlic, but it can be used in any form. Powder is easy to sprinkle on food, and freshly minced garlic is easy to mix in as well. To make it more palatable, sauté garlic in a little olive oil before mixing it with food, or crush it into a small amount of tamari soy sauce and allow to marinate for ten minutes. Then remove the garlic and top the cat's food with about an eighth of a teaspoon of the soy sauce. Just like people, some cats love garlic while others hate it. For kitties that turn up their nose at the smell, garlic supplements are available in pill form.

Like garlic, brewers yeast is said to make a cat's blood taste bad to fleas. You can find brewers yeast supplements at health food stores and some pet supply stores.

Herbs and plants such as eucalyptus, pennyroyal, rosemary, rue, and wormwood are said to have flea-fighting properties and they are often found on the ingredient lists of natural flea-control sprays, powders, shampoos, and collars. If you decide to try an herbal flea-control remedy, be aware that "natural" doesn't necessarily mean "safe." Any natural remedy can be toxic if used inappropriately or excessively. For instance, the oils of pennyroyal and citrus are toxic to cats and potentially fatal. Never put essential oils directly on a cat's skin. Note: don't confuse d-limonene, a citrus oil product, with citrus oil itself. Products containing d-limonene are safe for use on cats.

SMELLY SITUATION

My cat got sprayed by a skunk in our backyard. How do I get rid of that awful odor?

The day I saw my two cats sitting on our fenced patio, staring intently at a skunk, was the day I decided they would become strictly indoor cats. Luckily, I was able to coax them inside without incident, but if that hadn't been the case, I would have been heading to the grocery store to purchase tomato juice and Massengill douche. Yes, you read that correctly. Both of those products are said to be tops for removing skunk odor. Bathe your cat with regular shampoo, rinse, and then rinse her with either the tomato juice or the douche mixture. Rinse again thoroughly.

Another homemade remedy that can help remove skunk odor is a mixture of one teaspoon of your cat's regular shampoo and one-quarter cup of baking soda dissolved in one quart of 3 percent hydrogen peroxide. Thoroughly soak your cat with the mixture and then rinse her clean with warm water. Dispose of any remaining mixture.

You can also purchase commercial shampoos or sprays that are made to remove skunk odor. Look for them at pet supply stores or your veterinarian's office.

If you see your cat get sprayed, the first thing you should do is rinse her eyes, nose, and mouth with water to help prevent the irritation and inflammation that can be caused by the chemicals in a skunk's malodorous spray. If her eyes still look red or she's pawing at her face, take her to the veterinarian. He can make sure the eyes aren't damaged and prescribe a soothing ointment.

If skunks are common in your neck of the woods, keep your cat indoors (a good idea for a number of reasons). Skunks carry disease, including rabies, and they have more weapons than just their smell. A skunk's sharp claws and teeth can seriously injure your cat.

BATHING BEAUTIES

Will my cat ever need a bath?

Luckily for cats and people, cats don't need to be bathed very often. The exceptions are show cats, cats that have somehow managed to get very dirty, cats that have skin problems that must be treated with medicated shampoos, or cats that have had a run-in with a skunk. You may also want to bathe your cat frequently if you have allergies.

If you will be bathing your cat on a regular basis for show purposes or simply because you want to keep the level of dander in the environment low, it's best to start when she's a kitten and at least three months old. Use a gentle shampoo made specifically for cats.

Before bathing, brush the cat thoroughly to remove dead hair and mats, which will tangle even more when they get wet. Then gather everything you need for the bath—shampoo, towels, and cotton balls to place in the ears so water doesn't enter them. Some shampoos are concentrates that must be diluted with water. Prepare the mixture before you go get the cat.

The kitchen sink is a good place to bathe your cat, since it probably has a sprayer you can use to wet and rinse the cat. Put a rubber mat in the bottom of the sink so your cat won't slip and slide. Fill the sink about halfway with warm, not hot, water. Place your cat in the water, facing away from you to reduce the risk of being scratched. Don't forget to keep a firm hold on her! Some cats will squirm during the entire bath, while others settle into a resigned, sullen submission. Hold the head of the sprayer against your cat's body so she'll be less frightened by the sight or sound of the water. Be sure to sweet-talk your cat during the entire bathing process. Your calm, soothing voice telling her how good she is and how pretty she'll be will help her survive the indignity of it all.

Wet the cat down to the skin with warm water. (Be sure you test the temperature before you get the cat wet.) Lather with shampoo, being careful not to get soap in the eyes, then rinse the cat thoroughly with warm water. Repeat if the cat is really dirty or smelly. You can follow the shampoo with a crème rinse made for cats that will act as a detangler or softener. Rinse it thoroughly as well. Shampoo or crème rinse residue can irritate the skin and leave the coat looking dull, which defeats the purpose of giving the bath.

When you're through, drain the sink and dry the cat with a towel. You may go through two or three towels before you get most of the moisture out. If you have a brave cat, you can use a blow-dryer on a warm, gentle setting to complete the drying process. Hold the dryer at least a foot away from the cat so you don't burn the skin. Gently run a comb through the coat as you dry it to remove tangles and loose hairs. If a blow-dryer doesn't seem like a good idea, confine your cat to a warm place, away from drafts, until she's completely dry. For the finishing touch, brush the coat out. Give your cat a treat for being so patient.

FINDING A GROOMER

Giving a cat a bath or keeping a longhaired cat mat-free may be a task you'd rather leave to the professionals. The time and aggravation saved by having your cat professionally groomed can be well worth the expense, especially if you're trying to juggle a job, school, and kids along with cat care.

As with bathing, if you decide to have your cat professionally groomed, start when she's young. It's much easier for a groomer to teach a kitten to accept bathing and grooming procedures than it is to persuade an older cat that grooming is necessary. A good groomer can develop a relationship with a kitten that will last a lifetime.

When you're searching for a groomer, take just as much care as you would when selecting a veterinarian or other pet-care professional. Top-notch groomers not only treat their feline clients with love and respect, they also can spot potential health problems early on, and alert you that a visit to the veterinarian is in order. Before you choose a grooming shop out of the Yellow Pages or leave your cat at the grooming shop down the street, interview the groomer to make sure this is someone to whom you're willing to entrust your cat.

The best way to start your search is through that old standby, word of mouth. Ask your veterinarian if there's a groomer he or she recommends to clients. Some veterinarians even have groomers on staff. Your cat's breeder or cat-owning friends and neighbors are also good sources of recommendations. If all else fails, contact professional grooming organizations such as the American Grooming Shop Association for referrals. When you have some names, call each groomer for information about services offered, types of products used, and pricing. Some groomers offer pickup and delivery or make home visits in a specially equipped van, which can be a plus. Ask how long the groomer has been in business and what percentage of her clients is made up of cats.

Educational credentials are important too. Groomers may learn on the job by apprenticing with another groomer, or they may attend a grooming school. Following that, a groomer can become certified by one of the national certifying organizations. The law doesn't require certification, and many good groomers aren't certified, but the fact that a groomer is certified indicates that she's dedicated to improving her skills. If you find a groomer whose background suits you, visit the shop in person. It should be clean, neat, and well lit. Watch how the groomer and her staff handle the animals in their care. They should be firm but gentle. If you like what you see, make an appointment to bring Misty in for a bath and blowout. Groomers are trained, skilled professionals. By choosing carefully, you're sure to be pleased with your cat's appearance and the care she receives.

CHAPTER 10

Teaching Your New Cat

A COMMON MISCONCEPTION about cats is that they can't be trained. On the contrary, cats are very smart and respond well to training, especially when it starts in kittenhood. You can teach a cat just about anything you want. We taught all of our cats to come to the sound of a whistle, simply by whistling a particular tune every time we fed them. This form of associative training is called operant conditioning, and it works very well with cats. Many animal behaviorists now use clickers—small, handheld noisemakers—to teach cats any number of useful behaviors and fun tricks, from down and sit to walking on a leash and playing the piano.

"I've been quite pleasantly surprised with the number of my clients who have taken on the task of clicker-training their cats and have reaped tremendous benefits from it," says Alice Moon-Fanelli, PhD, a certified applied animal behaviorist and clinical assistant professor at Tufts School of Veterinary Medicine in Grafton, Massachusetts. "Both the owners and the cats have enjoyed the interaction and the mental stimulation and the fun of owning a cat that knows commands and does tricks."

Trick training is especially useful if you share your life with an Abyssinian or one of the Oriental breeds such as a Siamese, Balinese, or Javanese. These cats tend to be intelligent, inquisitive, and busy, so occupying them with training activities is rewarding for them and a sanity saver for you.

Another great reason for training your cat is so the two of you can do animal-assisted therapy. A number of cats enrich the lives of people at nursing homes and hospitals through their visits. A cat that can do tricks is even more welcome. Some of the basic behaviors you can teach your cat are sit, wave, give a paw, up, and off. Give your cat a really big reward for responding to the "off" command, Dr. Moon-Fanelli advises. It will come in handy when you find your vertically oriented companion on the dining room table, the kitchen counter, or any other high place you don't want her to be.

Cats are intelligent, sensitive animals who respond best to positive reinforcement. Yelling at them will get you nothing more than a bored yawn, and using force will really cause them to dig their paws in and refuse to do what you want. To teach your cat effectively, encourage and reward the behaviors you like, and ignore the ones you don't. Show him what you want him to do, and then persuade him to perform that behavior. The following questions and answers will help you develop a feline Einstein or, at the very least, a cat that mostly does what you want. And remember: teaching a cat properly in the first place is much easier than trying to correct bad habits.

CLICK, TREAT, CLICK, TREAT

I've heard about a technique called clicker training that can be used with any animal. Can I use it to teach my cat tricks?

Clicker training is a great way to teach cats tricks or other desirable behaviors. Clicker training guru Karen Pryor explains that using a clicker is like making a bargain with someone whose language you don't speak. The sound of the click identifies what you like and promises to pay for it with something the cat likes—usually a treat but also petting or praise. For instance, you might click every time you see your cat jumping onto his cat tree (click during the jump). Then give the cat a treat. After you've done this a few times, you'll have a cat that jumps onto the cat tree every time he sees you coming. At this point, you can add a word that identifies the action you want, such as "Up" or "Jump," or a hand signal that signifies the same thing, such as pointing a finger up.

Pryor describes clicker training as a game that you and your cat can play, a game that will improve your cat's health, activity level, and attitude. How? Clicker training gives your cat something to do besides eat and sleep, increases his interest in you, and lets him use his brain. It's a win-win situation. For your part, you're teaching your cat to come when he's called, to stay off the kitchen counter, or to give a high-five. From the cat's point of view, he's teaching you to click and give him treats, a satisfying state of feline affairs indeed. To learn more about how you can use clicker training to teach tricks and solve behavior problems, read Pryor's book *Getting Started: Clicker Training for Cats.*

SCRATCHING SOLUTIONS

My cat won't use his scratching post. I'm about ready to declaw him to protect my furnishings. Do you have any advice that will save his claws and my drapes?

All cats scratch, and it's important for them to do so (see chapter twelve for the reasons why). Rather than putting your cat through painful, unnecessary declawing surgery, take some simple steps to redirect your cat's scratching to his scratching post. To do this, you'll need a good scratching post—one that's at least three feet high and wrapped in rope or sisal, not carpet—some double-sided tape, and a spray bottle or squirt gun filled with water.

Use the tape to cover surfaces you don't want your cat to scratch. He won't like the feel of the tape and will look for an alternative. Place the scratching post near the furniture or drapes that he likes to scratch. Any time you see him scratching on the post, praise him and give him a treat. Encourage him to use the post by running your fingers up the post. The movement and sound will attract him. Another way to attract him to the post is to run a feather up and down it for him to chase. Between the praise, treats, and feather motion, your cat will quickly get the idea that using the scratching post is A Good Thing.

Where does the spray bottle or squirt gun come in? Leave several lying around the house, in areas where your cat tends to scratch on furniture or drapes. Any time you see him scratching on forbidden surfaces, give him a squirt with the water. Try not to let him see you doing this. He should think it's a bolt of lightning from the Big Cat in the Sky. The water won't hurt him, but it will startle him enough to make him stop scratching. At that point, take him to his post, encourage him to use it, and give praise and a treat when he does. Soon you'll be able to remove the double-stick tape, secure in the knowledge that your cat will use his post faithfully.

TOILET TRAINING

I saw a device at the pet store for teaching a cat to use a toilet instead of a litter box. Can this really be done?

People have successfully toilet trained cats. The only thing cats don't do is flush, although some manually dexterous cats could probably learn to add this to their repertoire. Toilet training a cat has a number of advantages, including not having to spend money on litter or scoop a litter box. It's probably easiest to accomplish if you start with a young cat and if you have a little-used bathroom that you can devote to the process.

I have never attempted this myself, so I won't presume to give instruction on the process, but there are at least a couple of books on the subject, including Eric Brotman's *How to Toilet Train Your Cat: The Education of Mango*, as well as the aforementioned device. Another great source for tips on toilet training a cat is Karawynn Long's Web site, www.karawynn.net/mishacat/toilet.html, where she explains how she toilet trained her cat Misha.

COMING WHEN CALLED

I want our cat to come when I call her, but my wife says cats aren't that smart. Is she right?

Your wife is behind the times. It's very easy to teach a cat to come to a particular signal, whether it's his name, a whistled tune, the ring of a bell, two sharp raps on a hard surface, or the sound of a can opener. We taught our cats to come by whistling as we set down their food bowls. Very quickly, they started coming at a run every time they heard that whistle. We only had to teach this to the first two cats, because as additional cats (and dogs) came along, they would copy the behavior.

Another way to teach a cat to come, using a clicker, is to give the signal you've chosen and then click any time the cat is coming toward you. Always be ready with a treat or a favorite toy to reinforce the behavior. Practice at different times of the day so your cat learns to come every time you give the signal, not just at mealtime. Don't use the clicker itself as the signal for your cat to come; it's strictly a way of telling your cat that he did the right thing and will be rewarded by a treat.

Never call your cat to come and then do something he dislikes, such as trimming his nails or giving him a bath. If you need to do those things, go and find him, and reward him with a treat afterward.

BEDTIME, NOT PLAYTIME

My kitten likes to play in the middle of the night. How can I teach her that we don't play at 2 a.m.?

Ah, yes, the 2 a.m. crazies. Your kitten will eventually grow out of this stage, but for now you need to make sure you wear her out before bedtime. If you see her sleeping during the day, wake her up and institute a rousing game of "chase the ping-pong ball" or "kill the feather toy." Continue this throughout the evening so she'll be ready to sleep when bedtime rolls around. If that doesn't work, you'll just have to ban her from the bedroom until she's sleeping through the night. Put her in her safe room and wish her sweet dreams, then head off to your own beauty rest.

BENEFITS OF EXERCISE

My cat is being really destructive and I don't know what to do about it. An article I read suggested that exercise would help, but how can that solve behavior problems?

Many behavior problems in cats can be traced to lack of exercise. Without sufficient exercise, cats get bored and frustrated because they have no outlet for their normal feline energy. Exercising your cat's body and mind with interactive toys, as well as interaction with you, can keep him entertained and less likely to engage in destructive behavior. Exercise and play reduce stress, provide aerobic exercise, improves motor skills, and enhances the bond you have with your cat. There's no downside to it.

NEW LEASH ON LIFE

I've heard that some cats can be leash trained to go on walks with their owners. Is this really possible?

Sure it is. Plenty of cats have made the journey to the dog side, learning to wear a halter and leash so they can safely enjoy the outdoors on supervised walks. Cats that are adventurous and sociable sorts, such as Siamese types, Abyssinians, Bengals, Bombays, Manx, and Ocicats do best with leash training, but any cat can learn. Once your cat adjusts to the feel of the harness—lots of cats think they can't walk with one on—and experiences the pleasures of a walk, he'll start asking for a daily outing, just like a dog does.

Teaching your cat to walk on a leash is a lot like teaching him to jump through hoops of fire: it can be done, but it's easier and less frustrating if you start with the right attitude. With a cat, the leash is there strictly as a safety device, not as a means of controlling his direction. If you start with the mind-set that the cat will be taking you for a stroll instead of the other way around, you'll be much more successful. As long as you have no firm destination and can avoid hazards, you should both have lots of fun and get some exercise at the same time.

Start by accustoming your cat to the harness. Why a harness instead of a collar? Cats are little Houdinis, and they can squirm out of a collar and head for the hills faster than you can imagine. A cat's neck is also more delicate than a dog's, so you don't want anything jerking on it.

Choose a sturdy, lightweight, figure-eight or figure H halter with one strap that fits around the cat's neck and another that passes around the body behind the forelegs. The metal ring in the center above the cat's back is where you attach the leash. Adjust the fit so that it's snug but not tight.

Once the harness is on, your cat will probably act as if he's paralyzed. He won't move, or he may even fall over. Ignore his dramatics and go on about your business. He needs time to figure out that the harness won't kill him and that he can, in fact, still walk. Give him as much time as he needs to get used to the feel of it on his body, leaving the harness on for ten minutes at a time, two or three times a day. Any time you see him standing up or moving while wearing the harness, give him a favorite treat. It should be something special that he doesn't get very often.

When your cat is accustomed to the harness, attach a lightweight five-foot or six-foot nylon or leather leash. Again, he'll need time to get used to the feel of it. Let him drag it around behind him for up to ten minutes at a time. If the leash gets caught on something, simply untangle it and let him go on his way. As you did before, give him a treat and praise him—"Good Oliver!"—any time you see him standing up or walking while the leash is attached. This first phase of training may take several weeks, so be patient.

Once Oliver decides that getting the treats and praise outweighs the annoyance of wearing the harness and leash, you're ready to try walking with him. Practice indoors at first. With the leash in your hand, standing slightly in front of your cat, show him a treat. If he walks toward you, give him the treat. Continue this as you move forward. After he starts getting the idea that following you is the thing to do when the leash is attached, you can begin giving fewer treats, gradually phasing them out altogether.

Any time your cat starts to go someplace you can't follow—or don't want to—just stop and stand still. Don't try to drag him in another direction. He'll learn that when the leash goes tight, he needs to move back toward you or in another direction. As always, give your cat a treat and praise when he does what you want. Ignore unwanted behavior, and don't give in to the temptation to say "No" or "Bad cat" or to physically make him do what you want. With cats, it has to be their idea.

When your cat walks readily on a leash indoors, you're ready for the big time: outside. Choose a quiet area with little traffic or noise. You don't want your cat to be distracted or frightened on his first venture. Your yard is a good place to start.

Let him go at his own pace, which more than likely will be slow and meandering, with intervals of butterfly chasing and rolling in a sunny spot in the grass. If your cat seems fearful, limit the walk to a couple of minutes. As he becomes accustomed to being outside, you can gradually extend the amount of time you walk. A good goal is ten minutes: five minutes one way and five minutes back. Being able to walk your cat can add a special dimension to your relationship, so be patient and positive while your cat is learning.

LEASH TRAINING TIPS

- If you have a kitten, begin leash training when she's five or six months old; it's easier to teach younger cats than older cats.
- Don't let your cat eat the grass in a public space or a neighbor's yard; it might be sprayed with pesticides.
- Be aware of potential hazards to your cat, especially approaching dogs. Pick your cat up if a dog approaches.
- Watch your step. Your cat may dart around your feet or cross in front of you as you walk.
- Attach a bell and ID tag to the harness in case your cat escapes you.
- If your cat is a walking fool, schedule outings at specific times so he knows when to expect them and doesn't cry to go outside at other times.

CHAPTER **11**

Exercise and Play for Your New Cat

PLAY OF ALL KINDS is integral to a kitten's healthy mental, emotional, and physical development. From solitary leaps and kicks to battling with a string toy to sliding across a slick floor after a ball, a kitten acquires agility, coordination, resourcefulness, and the ability to deal with the unexpected. He learns how to navigate the surrounding environment, racing up and down stairs, climbing the curtains, and falling into the water dish along the way. A kitten or cat that pounces on a ball or chases a feather toy is practicing his hunting techniques, substituting those objects for prey.

To keep his body and mind stimulated, provide your kitten or cat with interactive toys, live-action theater (window bird feeders), and if possible a floor-to-ceiling cat tree. "It's very important to supply this environmental enrichment, not only for physical well-being but also for psychological well-being," says Amy Marder, VMD. "Play fulfills a cat's predatory instinct and his need to have fun."

Play is also a sign of your kitten's or cat's good health. A kitten that's sick or undernourished doesn't have the energy to play and explore.

Knowing that play is normal behavior for kittens can help you recognize when something's wrong. If your kitten isn't inquisitive and mischievous, it's a good idea to take him to the veterinarian for an exam.

Regular playtime is especially important in single-cat households. Cats that don't have feline companions to run and wrestle with often display aggressive play behaviors toward their people, jumping out and biting or scratching them when they walk by. While most cats are willing to play for only a few minutes at a time, a playfully aggressive cat might demand ten or fifteen minutes of play two or three times a day. If your cat is healthy and willing, you can't overdo play or exercise. The following questions and answers will help you discover more ways to play with and exercise your cat.

LIVES TO EAT

My cat only wants to eat. Meals are the highlight of his day. How can I get him to play more?

Because cats are predators, often the most important thing in their lives is food. But regular exercise, in the form of play, not only burns calories, it also gives the cat something to look forward to other than food. A cat that becomes accustomed to play from an early age will look forward to it and will have less desire to eat obsessively. Try using food as a way to motivate your cat to play. There are lots of ways to combine exercise with your cat's love for food. Try hiding dry food under the corner of the sofa or in a paper towel roll or in a play and treat ball so he has to work to get it. Some people take whiffle balls and cut holes in them that are large enough to insert treats. As the cat bats the ball around, the treats fall out, rewarding the cat for play.

If your cat isn't obese (you don't want to stress his joints if he is), place his food dish on top of the refrigerator or some other high place so he has to jump up to get to it. (This also keeps the food dish out of reach of the dogs, which is an issue in some households.)

And, of course, while it's not exactly food, there's the old standby of toys scented with catnip, that herbal intoxicant that induces cats to roll, yowl, and kick while under its influence.

RUN, CHESSIE, RUN

My cat seems bored with her toys. What are some ways I can get her moving?

Being the predators that they are, cats are stimulated by movement. Use this instinct to give your cat some active play. The bouncing beam of a flashlight or laser pointer is often enough to excite the laziest of cats, and the fast, erratic motion enhances a cat's ability to think and move quickly. If a flashlight doesn't work, try a laser pen. Cats that won't chase flashlights will chase laser pens, probably because the pinpoint size looks like a bug. To give your cat a real workout, direct the light beam up and down the stairs or the cat tree, so he gets in plenty of running and jumping. A lot of cats enjoy tearing up and down the stairs, and it replaces running across yards outside. One way to encourage stair use is by placement of the litter box. Even if he doesn't get any other exercise, a cat will use the stairs several times a day going back and forth to the box. (Of course, for a senior cat, you need to make access to the litter box a little more convenient.)

Other toys that arouse a cat's desire to chase are formed like fishing poles, with flexible handles attached to lines with furry or feathery lures at the end. Dangle or drag this toy, and watch your cat become a silent stalker, ears forward and rear twitching, then pouncing on his prey, rolling and kicking to subdue it.

This is a great way to entertain your cat and keep him in shape.

ROUGH STUFF

My kitten scratches and bites when we play. How can I teach her to be more gentle?

Cats do play rough with each other, but they need to learn to take it easy with a human's delicate skin. Using your hands or fingers as play objects with kittens can cause biting and scratching behaviors to develop as the kitten matures. Instead, offer them a feather toy or fishing-pole toy that they can attack. Any time your kitten nabs you with her claws or teeth, loudly screech "Ouch!" and walk away, stopping the game. She'll soon learn to sheathe her claws and play gently if she wants your attention.

That said, my husband successfully came up with a way to "arm wrestle" with our cats—a game they all loved—that avoided this problem. He would place two or three thick athletic socks over his hand

and arm and then let the cats "wrestle" with the covered arm. As long as the socks were on, kicking and clawing were fair play. When the socks came off, the cats knew the game was over.

TOY ADDICT

My cat loves the fishing-pole toy. He sits in front of the closet crying until I bring it out. Is it all right for me to leave it for him to play with while I'm gone?

Most owners find that this is one toy that must be kept under lock and key when not in use or their cats will drag it out, chewing on the line and lure if no humans are around to operate it. String can be dangerous for cats to swallow, so this is one time when you need to put your foot down. Leave him some soft catnip toys or a treat ball instead, and save the fishing-pole toy for a special time in the evening after you come home from work.

KITTY PORN

I've been busy with our new baby and don't have as much time to play with the cat. Are there any other ways I can keep her exercised, entertained, and happy?

When people don't have time to go to the gym, they pop an exercise video into the VCR. You can do the same for your cat. No, not *Claws of Steel*, but one of the many specially made videos featuring birds, squirrels, and rabbits, whose movements and high-pitched sounds are brain candy for cats. Just make sure the TV won't fall over if your cat decides to leap at the screen in a vain attempt to score a meal. Look for these videos at pet supply stores.

For some cats, though, only the real thing is good enough. A bird feeder set into a window—with a one-way mirror so the cat can see out but the birds can't see in—will motivate just about any cat to jump into a window, teeth chattering in excitement. Your cat will be content to watch the birds for hours, plotting their destruction.

IN CASE OF INJURY

My cat thinks she's a trapeze artist, and the wild leaps she makes from and to high places worry me. Are there any signs of soreness or injury that I should be aware of?

Although cats often look as if they could teach yoga masters a thing or two, they aren't always the perfect athletes we make them out to be. Cats can fall off things or land improperly, so watch for signs of pain or injuries, such as lameness or unwillingness to play. Cats are reluctant to show signs of weakness, so these signs can be subtle. Take your cat to the veterinarian if the apparent soreness or limping continues beyond two days.

EXERCISE FOR THE WEIGHT-CHALLENGED CAT

The cat is one of the finest athletes of the animal world. Muscular and flexible, he's capable of leaping great heights or distances, of taking down fast-moving prey, of worming his way into the tiniest of spaces to explore. In our homes, though, cats have little opportunity to develop their athletic prowess. As stealthily as fog on little cat feet, weight creeps onto them. One day they're kittens in perpetual motion; the next, they're chubby cats who hardly seem to move at all, except from the bed to the food dish and back.

Overweight cats are prone to a number of health problems, including diabetes, hepatic lipidosis, and joint aches and pains, not to mention skin problems from their inability to reach and groom their backsides. On the flip side, a cat that gets plenty of play and exercise will be physically and mentally healthy: he's less likely to require trips to the veterinarian and less prone to destructive behavior problems, so keeping the pounds off with play and exercise should be a top priority, not only for your cat's health and your sanity, but also for your wallet's sake.

It's easy to implement a kitty exercise plan that takes only ten minutes a day. Schedule two five-minute indoor workouts in the morning and evening, or, if your cat is the adventurous type, plan a daily ten-minute walk on leash—five minutes in one direction and five minutes back home.

Exercise equipment costs won't bust your cat's budget. All you need are a fishing-pole-type toy; a small ball, such as a ping-pong ball; and a harness, leash, and collar if you're going for walks. A three-foot or higher scratching post is a plus, but not a necessity. If you can't find a fishing-pole toy, make one yourself by wadding up a piece of paper and tying a long string to it. Your cat will love it just the same. (Be sure to put string toys out of reach when playtime is over so they don't get chewed up or swallowed.)

Tailor the workout to your cat's physical condition. If he's middle-aged or old, overweight, inactive, and breathes heavily at the slightest exertion, get your veterinarian's okay before starting an exercise plan, and go slowly. Start with a gentle two-minute workout and gradually increase the time and amount of exertion as his condition improves.

Begin the workout with a few boxing moves to warm kitty up. Dangle the fishing pole above the cat's head so he will stand up and jab at it. Some cats will even do flips in their attempts to grab the lure.

Then move on to jogging. Entice your cat to run—or at least move at a fast pace—by dragging the pole behind you through the house. As your cat gets more fit, you can raise his level of exertion by encouraging him to chase the lure up onto the sofa or up and down the stairs. Another way to encourage climbing is to dangle the lure at the base of your cat's scratching post and slowly raise it toward the top.

Cats get bored easily, so at each session or on each day, alternate chasing the fishing lure with chasing a ball. Roll the ball on a tile or linoleum floor so that the noise and erratic movement will attract your cat. You can also roll it down the stairs or throw it in the bathtub—instant hockey rink! If you're lucky, your cat will have a tendency to retrieve the ball so you don't have to go after it, but if not, the exercise will probably do you good, too.

At some point, your cat will flop over onto his side or back. This is the signal that he's ready to do kitty crunches. Dangle the lure over his stomach so that he sits up to grab at it. Move the lure back toward his head to encourage him to lie down, then repeat until he gets bored.

That's all there is to it. End playtime with a scratch on the head and praise for being so playful. It won't be long before your cat is reminding you that it's time to go to the gym—the kitty gym, that is.

CHAPTER **12**

Your New Cat's Emotions, Social Needs, and Behavior

C ATS DO CRAZY THINGS sometimes. Or at least they seem crazy to us. To the cat, they're perfectly logical responses to his physical and emotional needs and his environment. Once you know how your cat perceives the world and why he acts the way he does, you can begin to communicate with him on a deeper level, especially if you are willing to make some adjustments to your own behavior. Understanding your cat's behavior begins with recognizing that he has feelings and emotions that are similar to but not the same as your own.

Like most animals, cats exhibit four basic survival behaviors: fight, flight, feeding, and reproduction. In addition, they experience such emotions as affection, anger, fear, frustration, happiness, pleasure, and sadness. For instance, cats clearly enjoy the company of a favorite person and, in extreme cases, become depressed or angry when that person is absent.

Cats also express themselves through physical displays, such as scratching, rubbing up against people or objects, and spraying urine.

These are all ways that cats communicate and define their territory. It's frustrating to deal with a cat that displays these behaviors inappropriately, but understanding why he does it is the key to solving the problem.

One of the ways cats mark their territory—including their people— is by rubbing up against objects.

Feline feelings are more limited in range than those of humans, and cats react differently than people to environmental stimuli, but there's no doubt that they have important emotional needs that when met can reinforce the special bond between human and cat. If you're starting with a kitten, the emotional issues you'll be dealing with are fairly simple and understandable: the kitten's bewilderment at being separated from his mother and littermates; his adjustment to a new home, people, and maybe even dogs; and, of course, the process of maturing into an adult cat.

The emotional issues you encounter after adopting an adult cat will vary depending on his background. Some cats suffer grief at the loss of their first family, which may have occurred because the owner died, a couple became divorced, or the family gave the cat up for whatever reason. This cat may take some time to adjust to his new home, or he may develop separation anxiety with his new people. Other cats may be fearful of men or children or dogs, based on past experiences, and will need help to overcome their antipathy.

Emotional needs and behavior go paw in paw with the need for socialization, that is, teaching your cat to be confident and curious, no matter what or who he encounters. A cat that's well socialized enjoys meeting new people, is easy to take to the veterinarian or groomer, can stay comfortably in a hotel when he's attending a cat show or traveling to a new home, accepts being boarded, and is startled but not fearful when he hears an unusual noise. He takes dogs and toddlers in stride, sure of his place in the world.

A good breeder will have already started the socialization process by handling kittens every day and raising them in a home environment so they become used to the sounds of vacuum cleaners, doorbells, blenders, and other household activity. You can continue the socialization process by introducing your kitten to car rides, dogs, and children, supervising carefully so the experience is a good one. When you take him to the veterinarian for the first time, schedule a visit with no vaccinations; you don't want his first association with the veterinarian to be a painful one.

If you're dealing with an adult cat, you can still work to help him become accustomed to new situations, places, and people. Take things slowly, and reward him with praise or a treat any time he reacts neutrally or positively to something or someone different. Ignore fearful behavior. Bringing attention to it or trying to soothe the cat will only reinforce his belief that there's definitely something to be afraid of. Other ways to help socialize a kitten or adult cat include establishing a daily routine and using play or grooming to divert the cat's attention from sounds or objects that induce fear.

The following questions and answers will help you understand your cat's emotions, social needs, and behavior, as well as suggest ways you can solve problems.

LONELY HEARTS CLUB

I sometimes worry that my cat is lonely when I'm at work during the day. Should I get her a friend?

Cats in general are territorial and solitary. While they can live peaceably in multiples and some prefer companionship, it's not something they always desire. If you really want to know if your cat is lonely or bored during the day, videotape her, advises Amy Marder, VMD, director of animal behavior services for the Animal Rescue League of Boston. "In all of my years of practice, when I've videotaped nonanxious animals that are left alone, they sleep. Cats spend a good part of the day sleeping, and most likely your cat is not looking for a companion during the day. If you do see signs that your cat would like companionship or is anxious when alone, such as pacing or vocalization, then a companion may be helpful."

PERK UP OLDER CAT

My older cat does nothing but sleep anymore. Should I get a kitten to help perk him up?

That depends on the individual cat. Bear in mind that it's normal for cats to sleep up to eighteen hours a day. You can perk your cat up just as much, if not more, by scheduling a regular playtime with him every day. Getting a second cat may just mean that you have two cats that sleep all day. And getting a kitten can do more to irritate than invig- orate an adult cat. Kittens have no manners, and they're very playful. Older cats don't have the intense motivation to play that a kitten does, and they can find kittens annoying, sometimes to the point that the older cat will develop behavior problems, such as spraying or not us- ing the litter box. If you decide to get a second cat, choose one that's reasonably close in age to your cat, especially if he's seven or more years old.

Go slowly when introducing the two cats. Confine one cat to a room—the safe room mentioned in chapter six, for instance—so they can meet first by smell rather than sight. Let them play footsy under the door. You may want to let them switch places for a few hours so that each cat can explore the other's area. Expect some general hiss- ing until they become accustomed to each other. If you're introduc- ing two adult cats, monitor them carefully until they establish a social order. Be sure you pay lots of attention to the cat whose territory now has to be shared.

WOOLLY BULLY

Why does my cat suck on all my sweaters? She's ruining them!

That's a good question. Some cats suck obsessively on items made of wool. Basically, it's a nursing behavior that may be caused by having been weaned too early, stress, or a lack of fiber in the cat's diet. This behavior is especially common in Siamese-type cats, although any cat can exhibit it.

If your cat is doing more than gentle sucking—actually putting holes in clothing or blankets, or ingesting wool—there are a few things you can try to eliminate or redirect the behavior. Add some fiber to her diet by growing some wheatgrass or oats that she can nibble on. Plain canned pumpkin (not the sweetened kind used in pies) is high in fiber and many cats enjoy the taste. Put a couple of teaspoons on her food at each meal. Every time you catch the cat sucking on something forbidden, distract her in some way, such as making an unusual noise. Don't appear to be paying any attention to her. When she stops sucking to see what's going on, remove the item and give her a toy, play with her, or groom her. Click and treat every time you see her sucking on a toy instead of clothing or bedding.

Note whether your cat sucks wool only at certain times. She may be doing it as a result of stress. Try to figure out what's stressing her, and change it if possible. If you can't, substitute grooming or playtime as described above in an effort to break the pattern. More frequent play and exercise can often help. Whatever you do, don't punish her.

For severe cases, or cases in which your cat moves on to sucking her own fur, your veterinarian may refer you to a veterinary behaviorist who can prescribe a drug that will reduce your cat's anxiety. Then you'll be better able to work on solving the underlying problem by modifying your cat's behavior using the above techniques. Drugs alone won't cure it.

MARKING TERRITORY

My male cat is spraying all over the house. What can I do to stop it?

One of the most common reasons that male cats spray is competition with other cats. He may feel threatened by another male in the household, or he may be telling cats roaming outside your home to go away—this is his place.

Neutering is the best solution for spraying. If your cat is neutered and the problem is with another cat in the household, you can help reduce the competition by separating the cats, or providing more litter boxes or feeding places. Sometimes cats, male and female, just like to mark their territory. Try putting their food in the area where they mark—they won't want to stink up their dining room. If the favored place to mark is a piece of furniture, you can try putting aluminum foil over the area where the cat sprays. He won't like the sound the urine makes when it hits the foil or the splashback effect.

Try using a Feliway diffuser to reduce your cat's need to mark. Feliway is a synthetic version of the pheromones secreted from glands on the cat's face. Cats use these pheromones to mark their territory, by rubbing their head on furniture, bedding, and even people. Pheromones aren't detectable by people, but to a cat they provide olfactory pleasure and a sense of comfort. Feliway comes in a spray preparation as well, but the diffuser provides a constant emission of the pheromones. Place it in the area where the cat likes to mark.

When the problem is with outdoor cats coming around, try reducing your cat's awareness of them by keeping doors, windows, and shades closed. You may also be able to rig some kind of booby trap that will keep intruding outdoor cats at bay by making noise or squirting them with water. If environmental changes don't help, drug therapy with Prozac or Paxil prescribed by a veterinary behaviorist can be effective.

SEPARATION ANXIETY

My cat pees on my pillow every time I leave for work. What's going on?

Although it's not as common—or at least, not as recognized—as it is in dogs, cats can develop separation anxiety. Cats with separation anxiety usually follow their favorite people everywhere. Lots of cats do that, but cats with separation anxiety react to the favored person's absence by misbehaving, sulking, or becoming depressed whenever they notice the person picking up keys or putting on a coat before leaving, refusing to eat, eliminating outside the litter box or spraying urine on the person's bed or clothing, or grooming themselves compulsively.

It's not often that you can cure separation anxiety, but you can manage it with attention, diversion, and sometimes medication. De-emphasize your comings and goings by making them calm and matter-of-fact. Don't fuss over your cat just before you leave, or she'll be more aware of the lack of attention after you're gone. Wait until you've been home for a few minutes before you feed your cat, pet her, or play with her. That way, she won't associate your return with these special activities.

The best thing you can do is to provide your cat with ways to entertain herself. She should have interesting toys, a climbing post, or a window bird feeder. Other ways to enrich your cat's environment while you're gone are to play a cat video featuring birds or fish, leave the television tuned to the Discovery Channel (a feline favorite), or play soft classical music on a radio or CD player.

READJUSTMENT AFTER SEPARATION

My cat seems angry with me after I return from a business trip. Why isn't he happy to see me?

Your cat may be feeling confusion rather than anger. Your absence created a change in his environment, to which he had to adjust. Now that you've returned, he needs to fit you back into his picture of the world. Perhaps it takes him a day or two to reestablish his bond with you and return to a normal routine.

THE COMFORT ZONE

My cat is easily stressed by any change in his environment. I'm not sure he needs Prozac or Paxil, but are there any natural remedies I can use to help him deal with stressful situations?

In addition to dealing with spraying, Feliway can be used in stressful situations such as riding in a car or airplane, or staying at the veterinary hospital. Spray it in the cat's cage or carrier to provide a soothing effect. Feliway can also help a cat adjust to a new home.

Besides Feliway, other natural substances can help calm cats that are unsettled, troubled, apprehensive, panicked, frightened, or unhappy. Bach flower remedies, prepared from the flowers of wild plants, bushes, and trees, were developed in the early twentieth century by a British physician, Edward Bach, to treat various states of mind, such as worry, indecision, hopelessness, or irritability. The remedies were developed for people, but they've been found to be useful for animals as well.

Try Mimulus or Aspen for cats that are fearful of being handled by strangers, such as at a new veterinary clinic, and Honeysuckle or Walnut for cats that are away from home or that are adjusting to life with a new family. Simply add two drops of the appropriate remedy to your cat's drinking water.

Whatever you try, remember that no remedy will resolve anxiety or inappropriate behavior on its own. You need to discover the root of the problem so you can deal with it through environmental change or behavior modification. The guidance of a qualified behaviorist may be necessary. In some cases, a cat simply needs time to adjust to new circumstances.

GREEN-EYED MONSTER

My cat seems to be jealous of my new girlfriend. Is there any way I can help these two ladies become friends?

Our cat Shelby fell in love with my husband on day one. As far as she was concerned, I was simply a necessary evil. The thing that brought her around was her love of a soft old plaid blanket. We discovered that Shelby would sit on the lap of whoever was covered with that blanket. She still preferred Jerry, but I became acceptable as long as I had that blanket.

As the newcomer in this ménage à trois, your girlfriend can start by not forcing her attentions on your cat. Instead, place some extra-special treats on the floor, roughly in a line from the cat to wherever your girlfriend is sitting. If your cat likes the treats enough, she may be willing to follow the treat trail, even though it brings her closer to the woman who's stealing her man's affections. Still not looking at the cat, your girlfriend can offer the cat some more treats when she's within arm's reach.

It may also help for your cat to see you and your girlfriend playing with one of the cat's favorite toys. She may even want to join in. If nothing else, the toy will now have your girlfriend's scent on it, helping to accustom your cat to her presence. These techniques can also work when cats appear to be afraid of people of a certain age (toddlers, for instance), gender, or ethnicity. In most such situations, patience and persistence—and sometimes an old red plaid blanket—will eventually win the day.

DECLAWING DILEMMA

My husband wants to declaw the cat to protect our furniture, but my sister says that's cruel. Is she right?

First of all, it's important to know that scratching is a normal behavior for cats. It helps them mark their territory through the scent that's released by the sebaceous glands in the paw pads.

More than that, scratching is physiologically necessary for cats. Cats are digitigrade animals, meaning that they walk on their toes. The toes help the foot meet the ground at a precise angle to keep the leg, shoulder, and back muscles and joints in the correct alignment. A cat uses his claws for balance, as well as to exercise and stretch the leg, back, shoulder, and paw muscles. He does this by digging his claws into a surface and pulling back, a movement that stretches and tones the muscles. Scratching keeps claws in shape, and it incorporates stretching. For cats, the act of scratching just plain feels good.

Feline advocates have long believed that declawing is a cruel and unnecessary surgery. Besides the physiological and psychological benefits of scratching, cats need their claws to defend themselves. A cat that is declawed can never be permitted to go outside, because he no longer has any way of protecting himself from predators.

A number of countries have banned declawing, including Australia, Austria, Brazil, Denmark, Finland, Germany, Great Britain, the Netherlands, New Zealand, Norway, and Sweden. In this country, the CFA disapproves of declawing, stating: "CFA perceives the declawing of cats (onychectomy) and the severing of digital tendons (tendonectomy) to be elective surgical procedures which are without benefit to the cat. Because of postoperative discomfort or pain, and potential future behavior or physical effects, CFA disapproves of declawing or tendonectomy surgery." CFA based its opinion on research and information from the Cornell Feline Health Center and the American Veterinary Medical Association, as well as interviews with veterinarians and feline behavioral specialists. According to the AVMA, inherent risks and complications of declawing surgery include anesthetic complications, hemorrhage, infection, and pain.

The reason declawing is considered cruel is because it involves amputating the last bone in the cat's toe: the distal phalanx. To remove the claw, the bone, nerve, joint capsule, collateral ligaments, and extensor and flexor tendons must all be removed. This alters the way the feet meet the ground and can cause problems with balance, as well as back pain. The equivalent in human terms would be the amputation of the last joint of a person's finger. Ethically, it's difficult to justify this kind of mutilation simply for an owner's convenience, especially when it's not difficult to teach a cat to use a scratching post. Instead of declawing your new cat, get her a great scratching post (or two) and teach her how to use it (see chapter ten).

That said, if the choice is between getting rid of the cat, keeping him outdoors, or declawing, then declawing is the best option.

GUILT COMPLEX

I came home last night to find that my cat had shredded my new chair. He took one look at me and slunk off. I'm sure he knew he did something wrong. Was he feeling guilty?

In a word, no. Guilt is an unknown emotion to cats. His behavior certainly seems to indicate a guilty conscience, but the reality is that your cat is simply a brilliant observer of human behavior. From past experience, he recognizes the signs that you're angry, and he knows that he'd better get out of Dodge until you've cooled off. It doesn't mean he knows why you're yelling at him or that he feels pangs of guilt for having destroyed the chair. The memory of that is long gone, even if it occurred just five minutes ago. Cats aren't capable of connecting past actions with present anger on your part.

Curb your anger, and try to figure out where you went wrong. Your cat may need a taller scratching post, more training on using the post, more playtime when you're home, or more diversions when you're gone.

FELINE BODY LANGUAGE

Cats communicate with us in every way they know how. They don't have speech as we understand it, but their facial expressions, body language, and vocalizations speak louder than words. Cats are good at telling us such things as when they're frightened, when they're suspicious, when they're angry, or when they're curious. Through observation, we can learn to interpret their actions and vocalizations and become fluent in the ancient language of the cat. Being able to understand what a cat is telling us forges a powerful link in the bond between people and cats. The following are a few signs a kitten or cat may display and what they mean.

- Active sleep. Kittens or cats that twitch, swish their tails, or vocalize during sleep are dreaming. We don't know what they're dreaming, but the brain is highly active during deep sleep periods.
- Crouching, ears low, whiskers back. On the defensive, this cat is ready to fight or take flight, whichever seems most advantageous.
- Ears up; whiskers standing straight out; alert, staring expression. This cat is on guard. He's telling an intruder to back off. If that doesn't work, he takes a more threatening position: back arched with tail straight up and bushed out so he looks bigger than he really is.
- Eyes (pupils) narrowed. A sign of aggression.
- Eyes (pupils) wide open. A cat prepared to defend himself.
- Head butt or face rub. A friendly greeting, but also a sign of possession. Cats have scent glands between their eyes and ears and on the chin and upper lip. When they rub their face

on a person or thing, they're declaring "This is mine" or "I like it here."

- Kneading with the paws. This cat is relaxed and content. The kneading action is reminiscent of the way kittens use their paws to express milk as they're nursing.
- Rolling. Cats bare their bellies as a display of trust, but also as a defensive measure—claws out and feet kicking. When a cat lets you rub his tummy, that's a good sign that he feels relaxed and is enjoying your attention.
- Scratching. Cats have scent glands on their paws, which serve to mark any area the cat scratches. The height of the scratch mark is also a message, the cat's way of showing how big he is, as a warning to any other cat that might try to invade his territory. That's why a tall scratching post, one that allows the cat to stretch out to his full height, is inviting to a cat.
- Slinking on the belly, tail dragging behind: This cat is exploring new territory and is taking precautions not to be seen. Cats in this posture may also be frightened.
- Tail up. "I'm king/queen of the world."

CHAPTER 13

Housetraining Your New Cat

C ATS INSTINCTIVELY HIDE their waste to cover up evidence of their presence. They were originally desert animals, so covering their waste with sand was a natural behavior, one that has become instinctive in their descendants. For your pampered house cat, the ideal place for a litter box is safe, clean, and quiet: no corners where he might feel trapped, no dogs bounding in hoping for a "snack," and no sudden or unexpected noises, such as a dryer buzzing or a garage door opening. All of these elements are key in teaching your cat to use a litter box.

The actual teaching part doesn't take much effort at all. Cats are genetically programmed to cover their scent by ritualistically burying it. Kittens can start learning to use a litter box at only a few weeks of age, as soon as they're able to move around. By the time you bring her home, it's likely that your kitten will have some familiarity with using a litter box. To reinforce her early training, find out what kind of litter she's been using. If possible, get some of that litter from the breeder and put it in your kitten's new litter box. Then place your kitten inside

the box. She might not use it right away, but the familiar scent will encourage her to return to it when she does need to go. Encourage the
kitten to use the litter box after every meal. Put her inside it and
scratch gently at the litter with your hand. The motion and sound
may stimulate her to eliminate right then and there. The idea is to get
your kitten to make the association between eating and then using
the litter box.

That doesn't mean, however, that it's a good idea to place the litter box in the same area where your cat eats. Your cat's dining area
and litter box should be as widely separated as possible. Cats don't
like to eat in the same place they eliminate; it offends their highly
sensitive noses.

The best spot for a litter box is a quiet place, away from household hustle and bustle. Lots of people choose the laundry room as
an ideal spot, but a washer going into a spin cycle or an untimely
buzzer from the dryer right when a cat is doing her business can
scare her away from the box for good. Consider an out-of-the-way
closet, a little-used bathroom, or an enclosed porch area with entry
through a cat door. Avoid rooms where a door can swing shut, trap-
ping the cat or preventing her from getting to her box.

There's always an element of vulnerability in using the box, so
your cat needs to feel safe from attack wherever you place it. Some
cats prefer a litter box that's out in the open, so they can keep an eye
on what's going on around them. A simple open box suits them just
fine. Others require more privacy. A covered litter box or one that's
inside a cabinet may be more to their taste. A covered box helps keep
litter contained and is a good choice for cats that like to spray urine.
Automated litter boxes rake out waste on a regular basis, but some
cats are frightened by the sound and movement of the rake, even
though they're not in the box at the time.

Whatever style you choose should be sturdy and well made.

Most litter boxes are made of heavy-duty plastic, so they're easy to clean and should last the cat's lifetime—a good ten to twenty years—although boxes with mechanical parts may have a shorter life span. Look for one that's easy to assemble—if it needs assembly. Whether mechanical or hand operated, parts should move smoothly.

If you have more than one cat, the rule of paw is to provide one box per cat plus one extra—keeping in mind that each cat may have different ideas about where the box should go. Experiment until you find placements that suit everyone. Don't line up the litter boxes next to each other. Cats will perceive this as only one litter box.

Does your home have two stories? Place a litter box on each floor. You want to make it convenient for your cat to use the box. This is even more important when your cat gets old. Cats can get arthritis, and they may no longer want to tromp up or down the stairs to get to the box. Don't make it difficult for your cat to potty in the right spot.

Once your kitten is using the litter box regularly, you can gradually switch to a different litter if you prefer another brand or type. Many cats dislike heavily scented litters or show a slight allergic reaction to the scent. Whenever possible, stick with plain litter, whether it's clumping, clay, or some other type. Gradually add the new litter to the box, mixing it with the old litter, over a period of a couple of weeks. (Cats aren't big on change.)

To keep your cat satisfied with the state of his litter box, scoop it daily. Scooping after every use is even better. Clean the inside of the box with a mild dish detergent every time you change the litter. Avoid cleansers or disinfectants that contain ammonia, pine oil, or phenolic compounds. After cleaning, dry the box thoroughly and put new litter inside it. Continue reading to find out more about the ins and outs of litter boxes.

The number-one way to ensure that your cat uses
the litter box is to keep it clean.

ALL ABOUT LITTER BOXES

What's the best litter box for my cat? I don't want to make any mistakes when I choose one.

The answer to this question depends a lot on the individual cat, as well as your own preferences. Among the factors to consider are the cat's age, size, elimination style, and privacy issues.

For a kitten, a basic open litter pan might be the best choice. It's inexpensive, easy to get into, and hard to miss when kitty is searching for a place to potty. It's easy to see when this box needs to be scooped, and there's no lid to remove, sifter to replace, or moving parts that can break. Using a liner cuts down on the necessity to clean the box every time you change the litter. This type of box is a good choice if your cat doesn't kick a lot when he's covering his waste, doesn't spray the side of the box, and doesn't mind peeing or pooping in the sight of all the world.

Consider a covered litter box if your cat appears to be digging to China as fast as he can when burying his waste. The high sides and lid will help keep litter inside the box no matter how much he kicks. To make scooping easier, some covered litter boxes have hoods that retract at the push of a button. Most have filters to help remove odors. Other features to look for include an entry step, which can make it easier for kittens or older cats to get inside, and a wide entrance to give the cat a feeling of security. And remember, with a covered litter box, you can't see if it needs to be scooped, so check it often to make sure it stays clean enough for your cat's finicky nature.

Finally, remember that the box you got for a kitten might not offer enough space for an adult cat. Consider upgrading him to a larger box if he's kicking a lot of litter out or having trouble maneuvering inside the box.

AUTOMATED CLEANUP

I've seen litter boxes that scoop automatically, and I think I'd like one. What are the pros and cons of this type of box?

This type of litter box (there are a couple of brands on the market now) is for the person who wants as little to do with the scooping process as possible. With the Litter Maid, a mechanized sifter goes into action ten minutes after the cat leaves a deposit, raking across the litter and depositing the waste in a receptacle. Then it goes back over the litter, leaving it as smooth and pristine as a Zen garden. The waste container lifts out and can simply be thrown away or emptied and reused. This model comes with a tent that keeps the cat from kicking litter out of the box as well as a ramp, which makes it easy for him to enter the box and removes litter from his feet as he exits. With tent, assembly takes half an hour to an hour. Avoid overfilling the Litter Maid, or the rake won't be able to do its job. The rake can also be thrown out of commission by a clump that's too large or sticks to the side, requiring removal with a scoop. It works with up to four cats, but is best for cats with perfect aim that stick to the center of the box. One drawback is that some cats are frightened by the motion or sound of the rake, even if they're not in the box at the time, and will begin avoiding it.

The Litter Robot has a space-age look, resembling R2-D2 or something out of *The Jetsons*. The cat enters the box and does his business. When he exits, a sensor is tripped, starting a seven-minute countdown. If the cat reenters the box during that time, the countdown restarts after the cat exits. After seven minutes, the globe rotates, sifting waste from clean litter and dumping it through the waste ports into a drawer inside the base. All you have to do is pull out the drawer and remove the waste bag.

The drawback to any automated litter box is the cost, which ranges from $160 to $350. They're available at pet supply stores, at mass merchandisers such as Wal-Mart, Target, and Kmart, by mail order, and online. If you're buying through mail order or online, don't forget to factor in the cost of shipping and handling. Or ask your local pet supply store to place a special order for you. For reviews of automated litter boxes by people who've used them, visit www.litterbox-central.com.

EASIER WAYS TO SCOOP

I hate scooping the litter box, but I can't afford to spend a couple of hundred dollars on one that's automated. Isn't there an easier way?

Something to take the mess and smell out of scooping poop has long been a dream of cat owners. Some styles of litter boxes don't entirely remove you from the stinky scene, but they make the experience a lot more user-friendly, even though they're not automated.

One is the Omega Paw, which I had doubts about when I first tried it. How could something that cost only $30 be self-cleaning? Granted, it's not truly automatic—operation requires you to roll the box forward so that waste collects in an internal grill and then falls into a removable tray—but it's way better than the alternative. To "reset" it, simply roll it back, making sure it goes far enough that the litter is redistributed over the entire box instead of remaining piled up at one end. Pull out the tray, dump the waste in the trash can, and slip the tray back into its slot. No need for liners, filters, or a scoop, and the cover keeps dust and odor to a minimum. Of course, you still need to clean the box on a regular basis. The Omega Paw works best with clumping litter. Sometimes the clumps get stuck and you need to bang on the side of the box to loosen them, but that's a minor flaw.

Some open-style litter boxes have screens that can be lifted out to sift waste. Simply remove it, dump the waste in the trash, and replace the screen. These boxes usually require you to replace the screen in an empty tray and pour the clean litter from the other tray on top of it, which can be a hassle.

You can also find sifting liners for the litter box. The directions say to place the entire stack of liners (usually a month's worth) in the litter box. Then fill the box with clumping litter. When the box needs to be scooped, remove the top liner, letting the clean litter sift through the holes. Toss the liner and the clumps of waste, and repeat as needed with the remaining liners.

A NEW LITTER BOX

I want to try a different style of litter box. How should I introduce my cat to the new box?

When switching to any new littler box, especially if it looks different from the one you already have, give your cat plenty of time to adjust to the change. Leave the old litter box out so Cashmere has the option of using it while she becomes accustomed to the presence of the new box. Unless the new box requires a different kind of litter, stick with the same brand and scent you've been using. Cats hate change, so make this one as easy as possible on them.

LITTER LARGESSE

There are so many different kinds of litter. What are the advantages and disadvantages of all of them? Is any one kind better than the others?

There's a reason for all those different types of cat litter. Each one caters to a specific niche in the overall market.

The widely available clay litter, the one that most everyone is familiar with, is inexpensive, absorbent, and readily available in grocery stores and pet supply stores. On the downside, it's dusty. It's also heavy, as you'll discover if you ever try to pick up a litter box filled with it. It gets stinky if it's not scooped frequently, and cats track it through the house, much to the dismay of the neatniks among us.

Clumping clay litter is easy to scoop and cats like the sandy texture. And believe me, when cats like a litter, that's a good thing. Clumping clay is also relatively inexpensive and is available in grocery stores and pet supply stores. On the other hand, it too can be dusty and cats track it through the house, although some brands are formulated to reduce tracking. Some brands are flushable, but if you flush the nonflushable kind down the toilet, you're going to have plumbing problems.

Litters that are based on paper, wood (pine or other wood pellets), or plants (wheat, corn, grass, alfalfa, peanut shells) are great for people who have allergies and need to keep dust levels low. Because they're biodegradable and flushable, they're also attractive to people who prefer to use environmentally "green" products. Some come in clumping formulations. Finally, on the plus side, they provide good odor control and absorbency, and the soft texture is easy on a cat's paws. On the minus side, they can be more expensive than clay litter. Some cats are put off by the texture if it's not what they're used to, and there can be some tracking.

Silica-based litter—the kind that looks like little round or oval crystals—is absorbent, dust-free, and biodegradable. It's also aesthetically pleasing. It is expensive, however, and some cats may not like the texture.

Finally, there's medical litter, which changes color if the pH level of a cat's urine rises, a warning sign of urinary tract disease. Another type of medical litter changes color if there is evidence of blood in the urine. You may want to use one of these litters if your cat is prone to urinary problems, some of which can be fatal if not caught in time. This type of litter is expensive and is available only from veterinarians.

CLUMPING CONCERNS

I've heard that clumping litter isn't safe for use with kittens. Why?

Many breeders are concerned that kittens who ingest clumping litter will develop intestinal blockages and die. They also believe that inhaling the dust from clumping litter is unhealthy. For these reasons, most breeders advise against using clumping litter with kittens. Their concerns may well be valid, but as of yet there are no documented cases of kittens dying from blockages after eating or inhaling clumping litter, only anecdotal reports.

TRACKING WOES

I have more than one cat. Is there any way to cut down on the amount of litter they track through the house?

Litter tracked through the house is definitely a major annoyance. If you're not already using one, try purchasing a low-tracking litter made for multiple-cat households. This type of litter usually comes in a clumping formulation.

Placing a mat of some kind in front of the litter box can also help reduce the amount of litter your cats track through the house. You can find specially made litter mats at the pet supply store or simply use a rubber door mat.

HIDING THE BOX

I live in a tiny studio apartment, and there's no out-of-the-way spot for the litter box. Is there some way I can camouflage it?

Not surprisingly, inventive cat owners have come up with some great ways to hide an unattractive litter box. You can often find cardboard covers at pet supply stores. These usually resemble cottages or castles or have some other decorative motif and fit over a litter box. They're nice because they not only hide the box, they also give the cat some privacy. They're lightweight, so they're easy to lift off for scooping. Sturdier and more decorative wicker covers are also available from mail-order catalogs.

If you go to a cat show, you can find actual furniture built to store the litter box and litter accessories. Usually in the form of a cabinet or end table, these pieces come in many finishes and styles to suit any décor. Their only downside is price, but if you can afford to spend a few hundred on a new piece of furniture, this could be the way to go.

CLEANING UP MISTAKES

My kitten didn't use the litter box. What's the best way to clean up the mess?

For potty accidents, keep on hand an enzymatic cleanser, which contains special enzymes that break down the proteins in urine and feces, removing odor and stains. This is important: if the cleanser doesn't remove the odor, your cat will return to the area, drawn by the scent, and use it again. Avoid cleansers that contain ammonia; it's a component of urine and will simply act as a scent beacon to the cat, luring him back to the spot. Club soda might work on stains, but it won't remove odor.

To clean up urine on carpet, use a couple of towels or rags to soak up as much of the liquid as possible. Then saturate the stain with the cleanser (I like Nature's Miracle or Odor Mute). Place a clean, dry towel over the area and top it with several heavy books. Their weight will help wick the moisture from the carpet. You can remove the books and towel after twenty-four hours, by which point the spot should be dry (or mostly dry) and odor- and stain-free. Follow the same procedure for feces, vomit, or hairballs, first removing as much of the solid mess as possible with a plastic bag or old towel.

ELIMINATION BEHAVIOR

My kitten stalks through the house making an odd cry and then uses the litter box. Is she in pain?

Kittens, like children, tend to announce when they're doing momentous things—such as pooping. Kittens often have a particular cry when they're searching for the litter box, and sometimes they accompany the cry with scooping motions using their front paws. This makes litter box training easy, because they're telling you very clearly what they need. If you show them where the box is once or twice, they're trained for life.

THINKING OUTSIDE THE BOX

My cat used to be really good about using his litter box, but lately he's been going outside it. How can I get him to start using the box again?

This requires a little detective work.

- Did you change the litter? Try going back to the previous brand or type.
- Have you moved the box? Put it back in its original spot and see if that solves the problem.
- Is another cat or dog bothering him while he's using the litter box? Put another box in a different area.

If these solutions don't work, take him to the veterinarian for an exam to rule out any health problems, such as a urinary tract infection.

Finally, you may need to retrain the cat to use the box. Place the litter box in a cage or a small room where the cat can be confined. Feed the cat and then put him in the cage or room until he uses the litter box. Continue this for at least two weeks until he uses the box consistently.

READING YOUR CAT'S HEALTH IN THE LITTER BOX

When is a litter box accident not an accident? When your cat is sick. Cats can't talk, so when they're not feeling well, they tell us in the most direct manner they know: they stop using the litter box. Following are some litter box clues that can indicate that your cat is sick, not stubborn.

- Urinating frequently in small amounts, especially in the corners of a room or other unusual locations.
- Squatting and straining for long periods.
- Passing bloody urine (if you have a light-colored carpet, you may notice pink stains where your cat has dribbled).
- Constantly licking at the vulva or penis.
- Crying out while urinating.

If your cat shows any of these signs, he may have cystitis, an infection of the bladder; feline lower urinary tract disease (FLUTD), the most common lower urinary tract disorder in cats; or bladder crystals.

All of these problems call for a visit to the veterinarian. FLUTD is especially serious, particularly in male cats. They can develop a plugged urethra, which can be fatal if not treated. Take your cat to the veterinarian if he shows any of these signs. To help prevent FLUTD, keep the litter box scrupulously clean, make sure your cat always has plenty of fresh water to drink, and don't let your cat get fat (excess weight can alter a cat's ability to urinate properly).

If your male cat is straining to urinate, he may have a urinary blockage, which can be fatal if not treated quickly. Female cats can have urethral blockages, too, but it's rare. Don't confuse urinary straining with constipation check to make sure your cat is producing urine. Other signs to watch for:

- Excessive thirst and urination. If your cat seems to be spending all his time in front of the water bowl, followed by frequent trips to the litter box, something is wrong. He could have diabetes or kidney disease.
- Diarrhea. This can be a sign of any number of problems and can be caused by such things as eating or drinking something unfamiliar, excitement or anxiety, bacterial or viral disease, ingestion of toxic substances, inflammatory bowel disease, or food allergies. Take your cat to the veterinarian if diarrhea continues for

more than twenty-four hours, especially if he's a kitten or an old cat. Diarrhea can rapidly dehydrate a cat.

- Constipation. It's normal for cats to produce one or two stools daily. Straining or pain during defecation, producing small, hard, dry stools, or defecating only every two or three days are all signs of constipation.

Possible causes of constipation include hairballs or other blockages, anxiety over being in a strange place, refusal to use a dirty litter box, or a condition called megacolon, in which the colon becomes enlarged and doesn't contract properly. Some Manx cats develop chronic constipation because of developmental deformities of the spine.

See your veterinarian if your cat is constipated. He may need a high-fiber diet, a hairball treatment, or a cleaner litter box.

CHAPTER 14

Traveling with Your New Cat

ALTHOUGH THEY HAVE a reputation as loners, most cats love to be with their people. You already know how training, exercise, and socialization can help build a bond with your cat, but did you know that many cats also enjoy travel? If it means they can be with their beloved human, cats will happily adapt to a life fueled by wanderlust, whether it's by car or RV, boat, or airplane. They are, after all, nomads at heart.

If you decide to travel with your cat, be sure to make hotel and—if applicable—air arrangements in advance. More and more hotels accept pets, but it's always a good idea to call ahead to confirm the policy. Don't rely on what a Web site or pet travel book says. Airlines limit the number of pets per flight, so your cat will need a reservation at the same time you make yours. Be prepared to pay a hefty fee (usually $75 each way) for the privilege, even though your cat isn't taking up a seat but is riding in a carrier stowed beneath the seat in front of you.

Other preparations include packing a bag that includes food and treats, bottled water to prevent tummy upset, grooming supplies, any regular medications your cat requires, and a favorite toy. Your veterinarian can provide you with a health certificate, which you may be required to present at the airport or at any state or international border crossings. I have yet to be asked for a health certificate for a pet, but of course the one time you go without something like that is the time you need it.

If you are moving or traveling with your cat, purchase a temporary write-on tag with your new phone number, your cell phone number, or the phone number of a friend or your veterinarian. Temporary tags are available at pet supply stores or from veterinarians or animal shelters. In the case of a move, provide your cat with an engraved ID tag that lists your new address and phone number on one side and a contact name and number in your previous neighborhood on the other. If your cat gets lost along the way, whoever finds her may not be able to reach you immediately at your new address.

When you're traveling by air and will be taking your cat in the cabin—a far safer choice than shipping her in cargo—purchase a soft-sided carrier that's roomy enough for your cat to stand up and turn around inside it. Not just any old tote bag will do; the bag must be approved by airlines for carry-on use. These bags are available at pet supply stores or by mail order. Look for such features as mesh panels with flaps that can be rolled up or down depending on whether your cat wants a view or privacy, top and front zippers for ease of placement and removal of the cat, a zippered end pocket (good for storing documents), an adjustable shoulder strap, and a coordinating accessory bag for holding medication or other items. The bag should wipe clean easily in case your cat has an accident inside it. Some bags have wheels for easier transport. The following questions and answers will help you travel successfully with your cat.

ROAD CAT

We travel frequently and would like to take our cat with us. Are cats good travelers?

That depends on the individual cat. Some are homebodies, but many are adventurous and don't care where they are as long as they're with their people. The best way to develop a cat that loves to travel is to introduce him to it at an early age. We frequently took our young cats on car rides around town when we were running errands at places that had drive-throughs, such as banks or fast-food restaurants. They loved it, and the early car socialization ensured that they took our two-day move to Arizona in stride. Cats are perfect RV companions, and if you have a station wagon or SUV, you can fix up the back area as your cat's place, using a harness and cross tie to keep her secure yet still allow her some freedom of movement. Always be sure that your cat is secured before you open the car or RV door; we almost lost Chessie in the Arizona desert when she decided to go on an unauthorized expedition.

AIR AFFAIR

We're moving to a new city and will be flying there. Should we tranquilize our cat for the flight?

That's generally not a good idea. Tranquilizers aren't recommended for use in animals that will be flying, according to the International Air Transport Association, because drugs can act differently at eight thousand feet above sea level, which is the approximate pressure in the cabin and cargo area during flight. Sedation in combination with increased altitude can also lower blood pressure, leaving the cat shaky and cold, create respiratory problems, and alter a cat's natural ability to balance and maintain equilibrium.

Instead, try using Rescue Remedy or Feliway, natural substances that don't have any side effects. Your presence, if the cat is traveling beneath your airline seat, will be the best tranquilizer of all. Many nervous cats settle down and go to sleep after a period of loud complaint, just to make sure you know how ill-treated they feel. To lessen the possibility of airsickness, limit food and water intake for several hours before the flight.

SHIPPING A CAT

Can we ship our cat by air to our new home?

If at all possible, avoid shipping your cat in the cargo bay. This is a stressful experience, given the loudness, turbulence, and possibility of other luggage falling on the crate. If for some reason your cat must fly baggage instead of in the cabin, you'll need a high-quality plastic crate that is airline approved. The information on sedation and feeding in the answer above also applies to cats flying in cargo. To provide liquid, place ice cubes in the dish that attaches to the inside of the crate door. Your cat can lick them if he's thirsty, and as they slowly melt they'll provide water.

Don't be shy about letting airline personnel such as desk agents and flight attendants know your cat is on the flight. The more people who know, the better. They'll be more likely to pay close attention to your cat's welfare if you've alerted them that he's on board. Give his name to the person who takes him at check-in so that he's personalized. Ask if you can watch him being loaded. If that's not possible, ask if there's a number you can call to track the flight and the cat's progress until he arrives at his destination. If you're on the same flight, ask the gate agent before you board the plane if he or she can track your cat's location so you can make sure he's safely on board.

Start early if you want your cat to be an enthusiastic traveler.

Any time the plane is delayed or you have any concerns about your cat's welfare, ask airline personnel to check on him. Your active involvement will help make the trip safer for him.

CAR TRAVEL

Our cat suffers from motion sickness, even on short car rides, and she'll be riding in the car for two days when we move to our new home. Are there any drugs that can help?

If natural remedies such as Rescue Remedy or Feliway don't work, ask your veterinarian about prescribing a drug such as buspirone, which prevents vomiting. A beneficial side effect for traveling cats is mild sedation. Buspirone goes to work about an hour and a half after the drug has entered the body by mouth, the amount of time required for the pill to get into the stomach, dissolve, be absorbed, and travel around the body. Whatever you give, don't use it right before you pack the cat in the car and expect it to work. Whether it's a natural product or a pharmaceutical, try it out a few days beforehand to make sure the dose is correct and that the cat doesn't have any reactions. Administer a drug an hour to an hour and a half before the trip begins.

BOARDING KENNEL VERSUS PET SITTER

We're going on a trip and can't take our cat along. Is it better to board him or to have a pet sitter come in to take care of him?

Cats are individuals, and what works well for one may be a disaster for another. Some cats love being boarded, while others prefer the comforts of home. If you have a very social cat, boarding may be the best solution. He'll enjoy watching everything that goes on around him, as well as the frequent interaction with kennel staff. Cats that are shy or introverted often do better in their own homes, where everything is familiar. As long as their food and water are provided daily and their litter box kept clean, they'd just as soon stay where they are, thank you very much. Aggressive cats may also be poor candidates for boarding.

No matter what your cat's personality, if you know he will need to be boarded at some point in his life, it's a good idea to introduce him to the concept when he's young. Schedule an occasional overnight or weekend stay at the kennel you choose so he can become accustomed to boarding stays while he's still at an adaptable age.

BOARDING KENNEL BASICS

What should I look for in a boarding kennel?

The ideal boarding kennel is comfortable and secure, with staff trained to monitor your cat for health problems, provide grooming as needed, and give your cat daily attention and supervision. Some boarding kennels are cats-only facilities, while others house dogs, birds, and other pets as well. In a multi-animal kennel, your cat will be housed in an area with other cats, not with dogs or other animals. Pluses to look for are a sunny window in each kennel for cat naps and a "kitty cam" so you can log on to the Internet to see how your cat is doing.

Put as much effort into finding a good kennel as you would a veterinarian or groomer. You can start by getting recommendations from your cat's breeder, your veterinarian, or cat-owning friends and neighbors. Check the Yellow Pages under Kennels.

Once you have some names, check with the Better Business Bureau to see if any complaints have been lodged against them. If not, make appointments to tour the kennels. Questions to ask include the following:

- Are you a member of the American Boarding Kennels Association? (This trade association promotes professional standards of pet care, requires members to follow a code of ethics, and offers voluntary facility accreditation.)
- Are you licensed or inspected by the state or city? (If a state requires licensing, the kennel will be required to post a current license or certificate showing that it meets the mandated standards.)
- Can you meet my cat's special needs? (Medication, a special diet, a given amount or type of attention or activity each day)
- What vaccinations do you require?
- How often are cats fed?
- Is someone at the facility twenty-four hours a day?
- Does the kennel have a veterinarian on staff or on call?
- How often is the litter box scooped?
- How far away is the litter box from the food and water dishes?
- What kind of bedding do you provide?

- Are cats housed away from dogs and kept separated from other cats?
- How are rates calculated?

Ask to see all the places your cat may be taken during his stay. As you tour the facility, use your nose and eyes. Does it look and smell clean? Is there sufficient ventilation and light? Is a comfortable temperature maintained? If you're satisfied with what you see and smell, as well as the answers you receive, then you've found your cat's home away from home.

Your veterinarian may offer boarding at her facility. This can be a plus because your cat will already be familiar with the place and the staff, but the drawback is that your cat may be exposed to other cats that are sick. Ask how healthy and sick cats are separated.

BEFORE BOARDING

Do I need to make any special preparations before taking my cat to the boarding kennel?

Just as you would if you were taking Oliver on a trip, pack a bag for him that contains a favorite toy, his own bedding (if that's what you prefer), any medications, food, or treats he'll need, and your veterinarian's phone number, your contact information, and the phone number of a backup person in case you can't be reached. If it's his first stay at the kennel you'll need to provide proof of vaccination. If you forget to bring it with you, your veterinarian may be willing to fax it to the kennel. Make sure the staff is aware of any medical or behavioral problems your cat has, such as diabetes or a fear of loud noises. Most of this information will be covered on the intake form the kennel will ask you to complete before checking your cat in. Just as you do at home, say good-bye to your cat matter-of-factly. Remember, if you're anxious or upset, he will be too.

FINDING A PET SITTER

I think my cat will be better off staying at home. What's the best way to find a pet sitter? Can I just ask my neighbor to come in and take care of my cat, or should I hire a professional?

There's more to pet sitting than providing basic care. Besides feeding and playing with your cat and scooping the litter box, a good pet sitter will keep a watchful eye on his health and emotional state. While asking a neighbor to take care of your cat while you're gone is convenient, your neighbor isn't necessarily qualified to give your cat the supervision he needs (unless she's also a cat owner or experienced with cats in general). Hiring a professional pet sitter ensures that an experienced person will show up every day to give your cat the attention and play he needs while you're gone. Most pet sitters also perform such daily tasks as bringing in mail and newspapers, watering plants, and turning lights on and off, giving your home a lived-in look.

Finding a reliable pet sitter who will visit your cat once or twice a day or even stay in your home allows you peace of mind when you must travel and your cat can't go. Start with the same steps you'd use to find a boarding kennel. Get recommendations and check the Yellow Pages under Pet Sitting Services. The veterinary technicians who work for your veterinarian may do pet sitting on the side. A vet tech is a great choice if your cat has special health needs, such as requiring regular medication or insulin injections. Other good sources of referrals are the National Association of Professional Pet Sitters (NAPPS) and Pet Sitters International (PSI), professional organizations that offer accreditation to pet sitters who meet their standards. You can find contact information for NAPPS and PSI in Appendix III.

When you have some names, set up interviews in your home so you can see how your cat reacts to the person. Look for someone who has professional experience, has completed pet-care study courses, is bonded and carries commercial liability insurance, and belongs to a professional organization. A pet sitter should have a brochure or other written material that details prices and services. He or she may ask you to sign a contract that spells out exactly what will be done. This protects both of you from misunderstandings.

Besides covering the above information, ask how your cat will be cared for in case something happens to the pet sitter. Ideally, the pet sitter will have a partner or some kind of contingency plan in the event of a personal emergency.

SEA CAT

Cats have a long history as sailors. For at least two thousand years, they've served as maritime rat catchers. The advantages of cats as boatmates are many. Cats are quiet, take up little space, are sure-footed, and can use a litter box. Taking your cat on board with you can be rewarding in a number of ways, but only if you're properly prepared.

Before you pack a duffle for Fluffy, take a trial run to make sure she's seaworthy. Not every cat adapts well to life on a boat. For instance, your cat should be amenable to life in confined quarters. Generally, this isn't a problem for cats, who sleep up to eighteen hours a day anyway.

Start by letting your cat become accustomed to the boat before you go out on the water. Spend a morning or afternoon just hanging out on the boat so your cat can familiarize herself with it. This is a good time to practice getting on and off the boat.

Even if they're leash trained, cats may find it unnerving to walk a gangplank, jump onto a thing that rocks when their paws hit it, or to be lifted onto this strange-looking "car." Take things slowly, and give lots of praise when she successfully makes it on board.

Keep your first trip short, no more than a couple of hours. This will give your cat an opportunity to get her sea legs, and you can find out if she's prone to seasickness. If Fluffy shows signs of having ship's cats as ancestors, the following tips will help you prepare her for life on board.

The number-one concern, of course, is safety. Until she gets her sea legs, a cat can easily fall overboard. A curious cat may even jump overboard if fish or dolphins attract her attention. A pet life preserver or a harness attached to a safety line can help keep your cat afloat until you can haul her out or even prevent her from going into the drink in the first place.

For greatest safety, your cat should wear a safety line. Run a jack line along the port and starboard sides of the boat and connect it by a ring to a safety line attached to the cat's harness. A cat that's leash trained will find it easier to adjust to wearing a safety line. For added safety, put up netting between the stanchions all the way around the boat. The best way to prevent "kitty overboard" incidents is simply to make a habit of knowing where your cat is. She doesn't know to yowl if she falls off, and it's possible you won't hear a splash, so keep a close eye on her until you're familiar with her habits.

If your cat does go overboard, you'll be less likely to panic if you're mentally prepared for the event and if you have confidence in the pet life preserver you've chosen. Test the life preserver before you need it. Put it on your cat to be sure it fits without obstructing movement and that she's comfortable wearing it. Some cats are put off by a life preserver's color or smell, so make sure she has time to get used to it. If the vest doesn't stay on or if the cat fights wearing it, it's not going to do any good.

Choose a vest with high visibility—bright yellow or orange—and a loop or handle for easy retrieval. Practice grabbing the loop or handle on the vest with a boat hook. It won't be long before Fluffy starts purring as soon as you pull the vest out because she knows she's going out on the boat.

Other safety precautions include hanging a rope ladder off the side. Cats are especially good at clambering up these. Keep a dip net handy, too. Last but not least, be sure your cat always wears a collar and tag with your name, the name of your boat, and the slip number.

The two primary physical needs your cat will face on board are eating and elimination. For the first, carry a good supply of your pet's regular food, especially if you're planning to visit foreign ports where it might not be available. If you start running out and won't have access to more for a while, begin mixing the cat's regular food with whatever you plan to feed him so his digestive system will have time to adjust. The last thing you want on a boat is a cat with diarrhea.

Stainless-steel food and water dishes are popular choices, since they're easy to clean and won't break. Some dishes are weighted at the bottom or angled outward so they won't slide around. You can also buy a specially made bowl with a lid on top and a hole in the middle for your cat to drink out of.

For potty breaks, all a cat needs is a litter box. Avoid using clumping litter. It hardens when it gets wet and is difficult to scrub off the deck.

Seasickness, sunburn, and skin problems are other concerns. Fortunately, seasickness seems to be rare, but if your Russian Blue does start looking a little green, a dose of Dramamine will usually take care of it. Ask your veterinarian what amount is appropriate for your cat's size.

Just like people, cats can become sunburned, especially if they have light-colored fur. The nose and ears are especially at risk. Monitor your cat's sun exposure, and make sure she has a shady place to retreat to. Apply sunscreen to the nose and ears for extra protection. Salt water can dry out your cat's fur and cause skin problems, so provide a freshwater rinse after any unplanned dunkings.

Most of the same injuries that happen to people on boats can happen to pets, so the supplies in the first-aid kit you carry can be used for your cat as well. It should include such things as material for bandages, antibiotic ointment, and saline solution for flushing out wounds.

Be sure your cat has a current health certificate from your veterinarian. It's unlikely that anyone will ask for it, but it's good to have, just in case, and it's required for Mexican ports. The incidence of rabies is higher in Mexico than in the United States, so a current vaccination is a must if your cat will be going ashore.

It's likely that your cat will be so fascinated by watching you, the birds, and the fish that she won't have time to get bored or destructive, but take a favorite toy or two along just in case things get slow.

Most marinas and yacht clubs welcome pets as long as they are well behaved. No matter where you're docked, the same rules of good pet ownership apply. Keep your cat leashed so she doesn't wander, and don't let her eat the parrot on the neighboring boat. Boaters tend to be early to bed, early to rise, so don't permit yowling or screeching after 9 p.m.

Afterword
Facing the Future
with Your New Cat

During the time I spent writing this book, I lost both my cats to old age and illness. They were fifteen and nineteen years old, good ages both, although of course I had hoped that their lives would continue for much longer. Their long life spans are a far cry from that of cats just a generation ago. When I was growing up, it was rare for a cat to reach her teens, let alone almost twenty. Cats these days, with their indoor lifestyles, high-quality food, and superb veterinary care have every chance of living to fifteen years or more. Some hit twenty and still keep going. Your new cat's senior years may seem far off, but you can start now to ensure that she will live a long and healthy life by keeping her indoors, giving her plenty of mental and physical stimulation, feeding her a healthy diet and preventing obesity, keeping her well groomed, observing her behavior and physical condition so you are aware of changes, and taking her for regular veterinary exams. When old age does creep up, the following tips will help you recognize the signs of aging, help your cat stay comfortable as her bones get creakier and her muscles stiffer, and finally, know when it's time to say good-bye.

WHEN IS YOUR CAT OLD?

Cats are individuals. Some starting showing signs of age as early as seven years, while others are kittenlike well into their teens. In general, however, a cat's geriatric years begin at eight to ten years of age. That's when the aging process begins to occur. Because cats spend so much time sleeping, we don't always notice that their activity level has decreased or that their movements are a little slower than they used to be. The aging process can be so gradual that it often takes an injury or illness to shock us into awareness.

RECOGNIZING THE SIGNS OF AGING

Rather than letting your cat's old age creep up on you, make it a habit to use your sense of sight, smell, and touch to become familiar with her well-being. You may notice that she's feeling a little bonier than usual when you pet her or that her breath isn't too appealing when she snuggles up to you on the sofa. If you notice these things, take a closer look at her overall condition. Changes you may notice include the following:

- Dry fur
- Flaky skin
- Thinning coat
- Slower movement
- Stiff joints
- Loss of muscle tone
- Weight loss
- Inactivity
- Worn or yellowing teeth
- Increased thirst
- Diminished hearing and vision
- Blue or gray pupils

What causes these signs? Age brings a decline in the metabolic rate. Tissues lose water and become more fibrous, causing stiffness in the joints and less elasticity in the skin, as well as flaky skin and dull fur. Fat edges out muscle as a percentage of body weight. Organs, such as the kidneys, pancreas, and thyroid, become less efficient, leading to reduced kidney function, diabetes, or hyperthyroidism. This slowing down and wearing out of the cat's body doesn't necessarily indicate serious problems, but it does mean that you need to pay closer attention to your cat's needs so you can limit the effects of some of these aging processes. For instance, regular brushing helps distribute body oils to keep the coat and skin conditioned, and even small amounts of exercise can reduce loss of muscle tone.

It's also a good idea to take your cat in for a geriatric exam. Disorders related to age can appear as early as eight to ten years of age. A geriatric exam, which includes lab work, assesses your cat's level of health and provides a baseline for future evaluations. To decide whether your cat is ready for a geriatric exam, ask yourself the following questions:

- Has my cat gained or lost more than a pound in the past year? Fat cats are more prone to disease, especially diabetes and congestive heart failure. Cats that are losing weight may be suffering from diabetes or hyperthyroidism.
- Does my cat vomit frequently, despite use of a hairball remedy? Frequent vomiting can be a sign of megaesophagus, hyperthyroidism, inflammatory bowel disease, or kidney disease.
- Is my cat drinking more water than usual? Excessive thirst—leading to more frequent urination—can indicate diabetes or kidney disease.
- Has my cat's appetite changed? If your cat isn't eating well, his teeth may hurt. Nibbling on dry food may be painful. In addi-

tion, lack of appetite or excessive appetite are signs of a number of diseases.

- Is my cat's stool hard and dry or soft? Is he straining to defecate? Constipated cats strain to defecate, or they produce a hard, dry stool. A soft stool or diarrhea can indicate intestinal disease or hyperthyroidism.

- Does my cat make frequent trips to the litter box to urinate, or is he urinating outside the litter box? Is there more or less urine than usual? Excessive urination usually occurs in conjunction with excessive thirst. It can indicate a bladder or kidney infection, or diabetes.

- Does my cat have bleeding gums, loose or broken teeth, or bad breath? Does she drop food while she's eating? Gum and teeth problems may be a sign of periodontal disease, which is common in cats.

- Is my cat's coat dry, dull, or flaky? Skin problems can indicate vitamin, mineral, or fatty acid deficiencies, as well as hormonal diseases, allergies, or parasites.

- Has my cat's energy level changed? Lack of energy can be a sign of many diseases, including anemia and cancer. Unusually high activity or agitation can indicate hyperthyroidism.

With the knowledge you and your veterinarian gain from the geriatric exam, you can take steps to prolong your cat's life and keep him comfortable and happy in his golden years. Once your cat is a senior citizen, consider scheduling veterinary exams twice a year to help ensure that you catch problems early.

DEALING WITH AGING

As your cat gets older, she'll slow down and take life easier. She may develop age-related health problems or be more interested in a nap than in turning flips as you dangle a feather toy for her to play with. She may have special nutritional needs. Nonetheless, life with an older cat is a special time. Here are some ways you can make things easier for your cat and for yourself.

The good news is that it's a great time for older cats. You can find special foods suited to their specific needs, new medications to treat common ailments, and products that can help them live more comfortably. Let's take a look at the problems that can affect older cats and what can be done about them.

Arthritis. This painful condition often goes unrecognized in cats, but it does occur, affecting the hips, elbows, and other joints. Cats with arthritis (or any painful condition) often try to hide it—maybe they know you'll take them to the veterinarian—so you have to look for subtle signs such as slowing down, no longer jumping up to high places, or refusing to climb stairs. Sometimes they seem stiff when they get up from a prone position. If your cat shows any of these signs, take her to the veterinarian. Ways to relieve musculoskeletal pain include weight loss, controlled activity, medication, acupuncture, and massage therapy.

Cancer. As cats age, they're more likely to develop cancer. Common types of cancer in cats include lymphosarcoma; mammary tumors in unspayed females; meningioma, a tumor of the central nervous system; squamous cell carcinoma in white cats; and ceruminous gland tumors, which originate in the glands that produce ear wax. A diagnosis of cancer used to be a death sentence, but improved diagnostic methods and treatment make survival common. Many forms of cancer are treatable with surgery or chemotherapy, especially if they're diagnosed early. Check your cat's body regularly for suspicious lumps or bumps that could indicate tumors, and be concerned about unexplained weight loss.

Cognitive Dysfunction Syndrome. Yes, cats can develop a condition similar to Alzheimer's disease in humans. Signs of CDS include disorientation (appearing lost or confused, or not recognizing familiar people or places), interacting less often with family members (no longer greeting people when they come home or refusing petting), sleep or activity changes (yowling or pacing in the middle of the night), and housetraining accidents. These signs are easily remembered with the acronym DISH. No drugs for CDS are approved for use in cats, but nutritional supplements containing choline may help to increase mental alertness.

Diabetes. This disease of the pancreas gland is a common and serious disorder in cats. It's caused by decreased insulin production of the pancreatic islet cells, or decreased responsiveness of the cat's body cells to the action of the insulin, rendering the body unable to use glucose for energy. Signs of diabetes are excessive thirst, increased urination, and weight loss despite a ravenous appetite. The disease can be controlled by diet and insulin injections. Our cat Peter was diagnosed with diabetes at age five and lived on to the ripe old age of fifteen.

Heart disease. Cardiomyopathy, or failure of the heart muscle, is a common condition in older cats. Signs of heart disease are lack of energy and appetite and a decreased activity level. If heart disease is diagnosed early, it can be managed with medication, so don't assume that your cat is simply slowing down from old age if she shows these signs.

Hyperthyroidism. The thyroid gland, located in the neck, secretes hormones (T_4 and T_3) that help regulate the body's metabolism. When thyroid levels become too high, the cat develops such signs as hyperactivity, sudden weight loss, increased appetite and stool volume, increased water intake, and increased urination. Hyperthyroidism is diagnosed with bloodwork, urinalysis, an electrocardiogram, and chest X-rays. It can be treated with medication, surgery, or radioactive iodine therapy, the latter being most effective.

Kidney disease. Early signs of kidney disease include a slight level of dehydration and a slight increase in urination and thirst. The cat's coat may look unkempt. Eventually, water consumption and volume of urine show a noticeable increase. Most common in cats seven years or older, kidney disease can usually be reversed or controlled with medication and a special diet, depending on the cause, the amount of damage, and the cat's response to treatment. Kidney failure, which is the most common cause of death in old cats, occurs when about 70 percent of kidney tissue is no longer functional. New tests allow veterinarians to diagnose kidney disease at a much earlier stage, and with treatment cats can have good quality of life for months or years.

Pain. The most common causes of pain in cats are surgery, trauma, dental disease, cancer, and arthritis. Fortunately, the past five years have brought advances in recognition of pain in cats, the ability to assess pain, and a better understanding of how cats respond to various types of pain-relief drugs. Although no pain medications in the United States are approved for use in cats, veterinarians have learned how to adapt drugs and dosing for use in cats. Nonpharmaceutical treatments such as acupuncture and massage can also help. Cats are good at masking pain, so be alert for any change in behavior, however minor, that might indicate pain, such as avoiding touch. Cats with dental pain will "chatter" if you raise the lip and gently rub the gums. They may also do this when they eat. The main challenges in treating pain in cats are recognizing it, finding an appropriate drug to treat the pain, and getting the cat to take a pill.

MAKING KITTY COMFORTABLE

You can take several steps to help your older cat stay happy and comfortable. She'll appreciate having a choice of warm spots to sleep. Place comfy beds around the house in sunny areas or near the fireplace.

If she's having trouble jumping up on furniture, make it easier for her by providing a ramp or step that she can use to access her favorite places. In a two-story house, place a litter box on each floor so she doesn't have to make a long trek up or down stairs to use it.

Grooming is more important than ever. Brushing stimulates the skin for good circulation, and it gives you an opportunity to check for lumps and bumps on or beneath the skin. Keep nails trimmed short; your cat may spend less time scratching as she ages. Other things to look for during a grooming session are bad breath, dirty ears, and runny eyes. Don't let these problems go unchecked; an older cat is less able to deal with what are seemingly minor health problems.

SAYING GOOD-BYE

Cats have nine lives, but they don't live forever, much as we might wish them to.

One of the most difficult decisions in your life will come when your cat is old or sick and no longer enjoying life. The kindest thing you can do is to release her from her suffering. A peaceful death is the best gift you can give to a cat who has provided many years of love and companionship.

How do you know when the time is right? That's an intensely personal decision, but if you can read the signals, your cat will let you know when it's time to let go. The main consideration is quality of life. Factors to consider include appetite, attitude, activity level, elimination habits, comfort, and interaction with family members. Does your cat have more good days than bad? Can she still do her favorite things? Does she act as if she's in pain?

Older cats spend most of their time eating, sleeping, going to the litter box, and getting attention. When they're not able to do those things, they're not enjoying life anymore. That's when you need to consider euthanasia.

Signs of deterioration can come on unexpectedly and quickly. A cat who has seemed to be getting along well may simply appear to give up one day, refusing to eat or move. The suddenness of this change sometimes means that you must make the decision to euthanize before you're really ready. It's a good idea to discuss the subject with the entire family and your veterinarian in advance so that everyone understands and agrees on the standards for quality of life. This is especially important if you have children.

Deciding to euthanize your cat is never an easy or clear-cut decision, but the question to ask yourself is whether you and your cat still enjoy each other's company. When the answer is no, you'll know it's time.

TEN WAYS TO KEEP YOUR NEW CAT HEALTHY AND HAPPY, EVEN WHEN SHE'S NO LONGER NEW

- Provide comfortable bedding.
- Make it easy for her to get on and off furniture.
- Make it easy for her to get to a litter box.
- Continue playing with her, even if it's at a reduced level.
- Maintain a weekly grooming schedule.
- Brush her teeth and don't neglect veterinary cleanings.
- Provide a high-quality diet.
- Consider switching her to canned food if she's having trouble eating dry food.
- Schedule regular veterinary visits.
- Include her in your family life and never stop loving her.

Appendix I
Cat Breeds

There are more than fifty cat breeds to choose from if you want something beyond the basic domestic shorthair or longhair (often abbreviated at shelters or in newspaper ads as DSH or DLH). The various types of pedigreed cats offer you a wide choice in personality, color, coat type, and body type. I've provided brief descriptions of forty-nine breeds, and you can learn more by consulting the *ASPCA Complete Guide to Cats* by James R. Richards, DVM, or visiting the CFA Web site at www.cfa.org.

Abyssinian: This active cat is people-oriented and very good at training people to do what he wants. He has a short, ticked tabby coat that comes in ruddy, red, blue, or fawn.

American Bobtail: Resembling a wild bobcat, the American Bobtail is a medium-size to large cat who is adaptable, devoted to his people, and friendly to all comers, including dogs. Often described as doglike, he enjoys playing games, including fetch.

American Curl: With his curled-back ears and plumed tail resembling a feather boa, the American Curl has a distinctive look. The Curl can have a long or short coat and requires minimal grooming. He's nicknamed the Peter Pan of cats for his lifelong exuberance.

American Shorthair: Created in North America from the working cats that came to this continent with early settlers, the American Shorthair comes in more than eighty different colors and patterns, including the striking brown patched tabby, the glistening blue-eyed white, the beautiful shaded silvers, smokes, and cameos, and the flashy calico van. They are differentiated from domestic shorthairs by their ability to produce kittens that are consistent in coat quality, body type, and personality.

American Wirehair: The American Wirehair breed began as a spontaneous mutation in a litter of upstate New York farm cats in 1966. His kinky coat (which can get greasy if not kept clean) distinguishes him from other breeds. In personality, he's described as quiet, reserved and loving.

Balinese: Originating as a spontaneous longhaired mutation of the Siamese cat, the Balinese is fun-loving and curious, but somewhat less vocal than his Siamese cousin. His long coat doesn't mat, and it comes in seal point, blue point, chocolate point, and lilac point.

Bengal: Created to be the domestic representation of a leopard, the Bengal has a striking spotted or marbled coat with thick, peltlike fur. He's active, intelligent, friendly, and assertive.

Birman: The Birman cat is believed to have originated in Burma, where he was considered sacred, the companion cat of the Kittah priests. He has a long, silky coat that doesn't mat and his personality is described as gentle, active, and playful, although he'll be quiet and unobtrusive if you are busy with other things.

Bombay: This black cat with copper eyes—described as a "parlor panther"—is congenial and intelligent. Bombays take well to leash training, enjoy playing fetch, and are endlessly inventive. They get along well with dogs and other pets.

British Shorthair: This breed is noted for his calm demeanor and loyalty to his family. He likes to supervise everything that's going on. His plush coat comes in many different colors and patterns and is easy to groom.

Burmese: These solid cats, sometimes described as "bricks wrapped in silk" because of their heft, are intelligent, charming, and talkative. Burmese are good with children and dogs and delight in spending time with their people. They will run the household if given half a chance. The Burmese has a short, easy-care coat that comes in sable, champagne, blue, and platinum.

European Burmese/Foreign Burmese: These are Burmese that come in colors other than those described above: red cream, seal tortie, blue tortie, chocolate tortie, and lilac tortie.

Burmilla: The result of a breeding between a lilac Burmese and a chinchilla Persian, the Burmilla is a sociable, playful cat that gets along well with children and dogs. Their short coats come in many different colors.

California Spangled Cat: Although he's strictly a domestic cat, the California Spangled has a wild look, thanks to his spotted coat. He enjoys the company of people and is sweet, smart, and active. This is a relatively new breed that was developed in the 1980s.

Chartreux: Often described as a "potato on toothpicks," the Chartreux has a robust body, broad shoulders and a deep chest, supported by medium short, finely boned legs. His medium-length blue fur has a woolly texture, and his eyes are a striking copper or gold color. He follows his people from room to room, has been known to play fetch, and has a reputation for being a fine mouser.

Colorpoint Siamese: a Siamese that comes in nontraditional colors, including tabby and tortoiseshell points.

Cornish Rex: With his large ears set high on a small, egg-shaped head, the Cornish Rex has been known to elicit the question "Is that cat from outer space?" Nope, he's from Cornwall, in Great Britain, where the first Cornish Rex appeared in a litter of barn cats in 1950. The Cornish Rex has a short, soft coat that has been compared to cut velvet, rabbit fur, or silk. He's an affectionate, active, people-oriented cat who loves to play games and participate in family life.

Cymric: A longhaired version of the Manx.

Devon Rex: Huge ears, a pixie-like face, and a coat of loose waves and curls distinguish the Devon Rex. The personality of this highly active cat has been described as a cross between that of a cat, a monkey, and Dennis the Menace. Devons like to jump and climb and are often found perched on an owner's shoulder. Minimal grooming keeps them looking good.

Egyptian Mau: This is the only natural spotted breed of domestic cat. The moderately active Mau (the Egyptian word for cat) is devoted to his people and will chortle in a soft, melodious voice when he's happy. Maus come in five colors: silver, bronze, smoke, black, and blue.

Exotic Shorthair: Sometimes referred to as the lazy man's Persian, the Exotic is simply a Persian wearing a short coat. The coat is thick, dense, and plush, giving the cat the look of a cuddly teddy bear.

Havana Brown: These mahogany-brown cats are highly intelligent and take well to leash training. They enjoy the company of people and will seek attention by tapping with a paw or rolling over for a tummy rub.

Highland Fold: A longhaired version of the Scottish Fold.

Himalayan: A Persian cat with Siamese coat colors.

Japanese Bobtail: The next time you see a ceramic cat with a raised paw beckoning from the window of a Japanese restaurant—the Japanese symbol for good luck—you will know that it's modeled after the Japanese Bobtail. These adaptable cats enjoy playing fetch, carrying things in their mouths, and riding on shoulders, get along well with children and dogs, and make good traveling companions. Any color except the Siamese pattern or Abyssinian-type agouti is permitted.

Javanese: This longhaired cat of Siamese type differs from the Balinese only in the colors accepted for championship competition. He looks elegant and refined, but in reality his body is hard, muscular, and strong, rendering him capable of great acrobatics. The Javanese is smart and likes to "talk," although his voice is softer than that of the Siamese. He's very good at using his paws and playing fetch. The silky coat is easy to care for as it doesn't mat. Colors include tortie point, red and cream point, and lynx point, with each having a distinct personality.

Korat: A symbol of good fortune in his homeland of Thailand, the gentle Korat is a beautiful silver color with luminous green eyes. He bonds closely with his people and enjoys cuddling.

LaPerm: Sporting a wavy coat that can vary from tight ringlets to long corkscrew curls, the gentle, affectionate LaPerm is an active breed that will learn tricks but also enjoys sitting in a lap. He comes in every recognized color and coat pattern.

Maine Coon: The Maine Coon is the native American longhaired cat and was recognized as a specific breed in Maine where he was held in high regard for his mousing talents. He's well known for his loving nature, kindly disposition and great intelligence. Maines are especially good with children and dogs. They come in all colors and patterns except for chocolate, lilac, and Siamese point patterns, and their long coat will mat if not brushed two or three times a week.

Manx: This cat is known for being tailless, but Manx kittens can have a full tail, a short tail, a rise (known as a rumpy riser), or no tail (rumpy). Breeders may end up with all of these tail lengths in a single litter. The playful Manx is a superb jumper and loves observing his surroundings from the highest point in the room. When he's not up high, he might be retrieving or burying his toys, in much the same way as a dog. Manx bond closely with their people.

Nebelung: A longhaired Russian Blue.

Norwegian Forest Cat: The people-oriented skogkatt, meaning forest cat, originated in Scandinavia. He has bright emerald green eyes with a band of gold, long flowing hair, a sweet expression, and jaunty ear and toe trimmings. The coat comes in most colors, from pure white to coal black, with many coat patterns and color combinations in between, with the exception of the colorpoint colors. Little combing is required for non-show cats, but it is recommended during spring shedding.

Ocicat: An agouti spotted cat of moderate type, the Ocicat was developed by interbreeding Abyssinians, Siamese, and American Shorthairs. Ocicats are large, active, and athletic, with a short, shiny coat. Confident and extroverted, they are easily trained and will walk on leash, play fetch, and respond to voice commands. They enjoy the companionship of people and other animals, adapt well to travel, and are easy to groom.

Oriental: The sleek Oriental has an angular head, large flaring ears, a svelte, tubular body, and tall, slender legs. Curious and intelligent, he craves attention and affection and will greet his people when they arrive home, eager to tell them about his day, which he probably spent opening and emptying drawers in search of fun toys. This nonpointed Siamese type comes in many color and pattern combinations.

Persian: His sweet, gentle personality and long, flowing coat has made the Persian the number one breed in popularity. This is a laid-back cat who appreciates serenity and security, but in the care of a loving family he can adapt to the most boisterous of households. The Persian's long, flowing coat, which comes in an astonishing number of colors, needs daily combing to prevent tangles and hairballs.

Ragamuffin: A gorgeous, massive cat weighing ten to twenty pounds, the Ragamuffin is sweet and people-oriented, following family members from room to room to supervise and participate in their doings. Calm and patient, they are good with kids and are often found attending tea parties or taking rides in baby strollers. The breed comes in all coat colors and patterns, including blue, brown tabby with white, tortoiseshell, and mink. The thick, plush coat is medium long, but it doesn't readily mat or clump and is easy to care for.

Ragdoll: Large, loving, and laid back, the Ragdoll is a longhaired cat with a light-colored body, darker points on the face, legs, tail, and ears, and big blue eyes. He comes in four patterns: bicolor, van, mitted, and pointed. The patterns come in six colors: seal, blue, chocolate, lilac, red, and cream. Points may be solid, lynx, or tortie. This gentle breed adores people and gets along well with kids and dogs. Ragdolls make good therapy cats as well.

Russian Blue: This gentle, affectionate cat has a short, dense blue coat with silver tipping and vivid green eyes. The wedge-shaped head is topped with large, pointed ears. He's a quiet cat with a devoted nature who is smart enough to open doors and teach his people to fetch. He gets along well with children and other pets and requires minimal grooming.

Scottish Fold: With ears folded forward and downward on the head, the Scottish Fold has been described as having the look of a pixie, owl, or teddy bear. Scottish Folds come in two types: folded ear and straight (normal) ear. The folded ear is produced by an incomplete dominant gene and is the result of a spontaneous mutation. Scottish Folds adapt to almost any home situation and are comfortable in a room full of noisy children and dogs. They come in any and all colors, with the exception of those showing evidence of hybridization, such as chocolate, lavender, the Himalayan pattern, or a combination of these and white.

Selkirk Rex: One of the newest natural breeds, the Selkirk Rex is being developed as a large, heavy boned cat. He has curly whiskers and a plush, loosely curled coat that comes in short or long lengths. Both curly and straight-haired kittens can appear in a single litter. Selkirk Rex are patient, loving, and tolerant cats who excel at making their people laugh.

Siamese: Hailing from Thailand, or Siam, as it was once known, the Siamese has dramatic looks and a dramatic personality. His short, light-colored coat is set off by darker points on the legs, tail, and ears, as well as a dark mask. A long wedge-shaped head, elongated body, and deep blue almond-shaped eyes complete the picture. The Siamese spends as much time as possible with his people, conversing with them loudly and at length.

Siberian: The national cat of Russia, the Siberian has a medium-length coat that is rich and full in winter and somewhat less dense in summer. He comes in just about any color, but because he's so rare, not all colors are always available. This people-loving cat is agile and has been known to leap great distances and heights. He is described as a good problem solver, meaning his people need to be on the ball to stay one step ahead of him.

Singapura: The small, shorthaired Singapura originated on the streets of Singapore and was developed as a breed in the 1970s. He has noticeably large eyes and ears and a ticked, light beige coat that resembles that of a cougar. The Singapura is extroverted, curious, and playful, and he wants to help his people with everything they're do-ing. This cat is a jumper, so look up high when he seems to have dis-appeared.

Snowshoe: Descending from the American Shorthair and the Siamese, the Snowshoe has a short coat with a pointed pattern, white markings on the feet, and an inverted white V on the face. He comes in two color combinations: seal point and white, and blue point and white. The people-oriented Snowshoe is affectionate and easygoing, getting along well with children and other pets.

Somali: This cat is a longhaired version of the Abyssinian. With his large ears, masked face, full ruff, and bushy tail, he resembles a small fox. He's an active cat that enjoys tossing balls and toys in the air, playing fetch, and manipulating things, especially water faucets, with his paws. The Somali's medium-length agouti coat is easy to care for and comes in four colors: ruddy, red, blue, and fawn.

Sphynx: This hairless cat, who feels like suede to the touch, is the result of a natural mutation and was developed in the 1960s. His sturdy, muscular body is covered with a fine down, and he comes in a variety of colors, seen in the pigment of the skin and in the few hairs that are often found on the nose, tail, and toes. He has a wide-eyed, intelligent expression and loves to be the center of attention—and will perform silly antics to get it. If he gets cold, the Sphynx will cud-dle up with a warm person, a dog, or another cat.

Tonkinese: Smart, strong-willed, and inventive, the Tonkinese is an excellent house and family manager who loves being in a lap or rid-ing on a shoulder, supervising everything that goes on. He'll play fetch with his favorite toys and plays tag or hide and seek with other cats or his people. Expect him to greet guests at the door and then entertain them with his acrobatics. Tonkinese come in a variety of colors and patterns.

Turkish Angora: This intelligent and devoted cat has a long, elegant body and a silky medium-length coat that comes in a variety of colors and patterns, including solids, tabbies, smokes, and parti-colors. Filled with a zest for life, they enjoy running and playing, and their beautiful coat is easy to groom.

Turkish Van: Known as the swimming cat in his native region of central and southwest Asia, the Turkish Van is distinguished by his love of water and his medium-length piebald, or van, coat: white with colored markings restricted primarily to the head and tail. The coat isn't prone to matting, so it's easy to care for. This is a high-energy cat who's smart and affectionate.

York Chocolate: This is a new breed, developed in the 1980s in New York State. His medium-length silky coat is solid or bicolored in chocolate or lilac, and he has a plumed tail, toe tufts, and a moderate neck ruff. These cats are smart and energetic, but they also love to sit in a lap.

Appendix II
Sample Adoption Contract

Here is an adoption contract that illustrates what animal shelters and breed rescue groups require from adopters of the kittens and cats in their care. But, while this contract is quite typical, it is not reproducible—unless you obtain the written consent of the organization that allowed us to use the contract for this book.

ADOPTION CONTRACT
Hillside SPCA Animal Shelter
Schuylkill County, Pennsylvania

Adoption Contract/Guidelines

This is our standard adoption contract that must be completed and signed by anyone wishing to adopt an animal from the Hillside SPCA. Our number one concern is for the animals and we strive to place them in good, loving homes.

Please NOTE: We DO NOT refund adoption fees—no exceptions.

Adoption Contract

All animal adoption contracts approved by the Hillside S.P.C.A., Inc. are subject to the following terms and conditions:

1. The Adopter agrees that the animal will be kept only as a domesticated house pet. This means that dogs will be kept indoors except for periods of exercise in a fenced-in yard or on a leash. Cats will be kept indoors at all times unless a screened-in porch or similar type enclosure is available.

2. The adopter agrees to have the animal spayed or neutered by the date specified above. The Adopter further agrees to provide proper veterinary care for the animal.

3. The Adopter grants the Hillside S.P.C.A., Inc. the right to make periodic visits to the Adopter's premises for the purpose of checking on the health and general welfare of the animal and to verify that the animal has been spayed or neutered in accordance with the terms of this agreement.

4. The Adopter represents that all family members have agreed to the adoption of the animal and that all family members will abide by the terms of this agreement. The Adopter further represents that he/she is eighteen years of age or older.

5. The Adopter represents that he/she has never been subject to legal action for cruelty to or neglect of animals. The Adopter further represents that he/she has never owned an animal which has been confiscated by any animal control or humane organization for violations of state or local animal control regulations or animal adoption agreements.

6. If the Adopter is a tenant, then Adopter agrees to provide written permission from the landlord consenting to the animal adoption.

7. If for any reason the Adopter is unable to provide care to the animal, the Adopter agrees to return the animal to the Hillside S.P.C.A., Inc. The Adopter shall not offer the animal for sale or give the animal to any third party without the prior written consent of the Hillside S.P.C.A., Inc.

8. The Adopter agrees that the Hillside S.P.C.A., Inc. shall have the right of immediate possession of the animal if, in the judgment of the Hillside S.P.C.A.,

Inc. the animal is receiving inadequate care, is being improperly housed or handled or has not been spayed or neutered by the specified date.

9. The Adopter agrees to pay the Hillside S.P.C.A., Inc. the sum of $300.000 as liquidated damages in the event the terms of this contract are breached; this liquidated damage value does not bar the Hillside S.P.C.A., Inc. from seeking the return of the animal by judicial process or other legal means if necessary. If legal action is instituted, the Adopter agrees to pay reasonable attorney's fees and court costs.

10. The Adopter hereby declares that he/she is aware: (a) That animals are different from human beings in their responses to human actions; (b) That the actions of animals are often unpredictable. (c) That an animal's behavior may change after it leaves the shelter and accustoms itself to a home or other different environment; and (d) That the Hillside S.P.C.A., Inc. makes no claims as to the temperament, health, or mental disposition of any animal put up for adoption.

11. The Adopter understands that there will be NO REFUNDS OF ADOPTION FEE.

12. The Adopter acknowledges that he/she has received a copy of the Hillside S.P.C.A., Inc. Animal Adoption Contract Terms.

13. The Adopter hereby accepts possession of, title to (subjec to the conditions of the adoption contract), and responsibility for the animal adopted and agrees to release and discharge the Hillside S.P.C.A., Inc. forever from liability for any injury or damages to any person or property caused by the adopted animal, and from any causes of action, claims, suits, or demands whatsoever that may arise as a result of such injury or damages.

Appendix III
Resources

Books

ASPCA Complete Guide to Cats, James R. Richards, DVM, Chronicle Books, 2001

A Cat Is Watching, Roger Caras, Fireside Books, 1990

Cat Owner's Home Veterinary Handbook, Delbert G. Carlson, DVM, and James M. Giffin, MD, Howell Book House, 1995

Getting Started: Clicker Training for Cats, Karen Pryor, Sunshine Books, 2001

Communicating with Your Cat, J. Anne Helgren, Barrons, 1999

The Cornell Book of Cats, edited by Mordecai Siegal, Villard, 1997

Hiss and Tell: True Stories from the Files of a Cat Shrink, Pam Johnson-Bennett, Penguin, 2001

How to Toilet Train Your Cat: The Education of Mango, Eric Brotman, 2001

The Humane Society of the United States Complete Guide to Cat Care, Wendy Christensen, St. Martin's Press, 2002

New Choices in Natural Healing for Dogs and Cats, Amy D. Shojai, Rodale Press, 2001

Pet Care in the New Century: Cutting-Edge Medicine for Dogs and Cats, Amy D. Shojai, New American Library, 2001

Organizations

American Association of Cat Enthusiasts, PO Box 213, Pine Brook, New
Jersey 07058; (973) 335–6717; www.aaceinc.org

American Cat Fanciers Association, PO Box 1949, Nixa, Missouri 65714–1949;
(417) 725–1530; www.acfacat.com

ASPCA Animal Poison Control Center, 1717 S. Philo, Ste. 36, Urbana, Illi-
nois 61802, (888) 426–4435; www.napcc.aspca.org

Canadian Cat Association, 289 Rutherford Rd. S., Unit 18, Brampton, On-
tario, Canada L6W 3R9; (905) 459–1481; www.cca-afc.com

Cat Fanciers Association, PO Box 1005, Manasquan, New Jersey 08736–0805;
(732) 528–9797; www.cfainc.org

Love On A Leash: The Foundation for Pet-Provided Therapy, PO Box 6308,
Oceanside, California 92058; (760) 740–2326; www.loveonaleash.org

National Association of Professional Pet Sitters, 17000 Commerce Pkwy.,
Ste. C, Mt. Laurel, New Jersey 08054, (800) 296–7387; www.petsitters.org

Orthopedic Foundation for Animals, 2300 E. Nifong Blvd., Columbia, Missouri 65201; www.offa.org

PetCare Insurance, 3315 E. Algonquin Rd., Ste. 450, Rolling Meadows, Illi-
nois 60008; (866) 275–7387 (toll-free); www.petcareinsurance.com

Pet Sitters International, 201 E. King St., King, North Carolina 27021–9161;
(336) 983–9222; www.petsit.com

Veterinary Pet Insurance, PO Box 2344, Brea, California 92822–2344; (800)
USA-PETS; www.petinsurance.com

Publications

Catnip. A monthly newsletter published in conjunction with the Tufts University School of Veterinary Medicine. The magazine focuses on presenting cat owners with the latest information on feline medicine,
health, and behavior. Yearly subscription is $39. Catnip, PO Box 420070,
Palm Coast, Florida 32142–9571

CatWatch. A monthly newsletter published in conjunction with Cornell
University College of Veterinary Medicine. Yearly subscription is $39.
CatWatch, PO Box 42035, Palm Coast, Florida 32142–0235

Web Sites

www.altvetmed.com

www.americanhumane.org, American Humane Association

www.arlboston.com, Animal Rescue League of Boston, Massachusetts

www.breedlist.com

www.cats.about.com/mbody.htm

www.cathelp-online.com

www.fabcats.org, Feline Advisory Bureau

www.fanciers.com

www.litterbox-central.com

www.meowhoo.com

www.petfinder.com

www.petfooddirect.com

www.petplace.com

www.petsforlife.org, The Humane Society of the United States

www.sfspca.org, San Francisco SPCA

www.thecatsite.com

www.thedailycat.com

www.tica.org, The International Cat Association

www.traditionalcats.com, Traditional Cat Association

Index